RESTORATIVE JUSTICE UP CLOSE

RESTORATIVE JUSTICE UP CLOSE

First-Person Accounts of an Approach That Works

Edited by
Sally Swarthout Wolf

THE
NEW
PRESS

NEW YORK
LONDON

Requests for permission to reproduce selections from this book should be made
through our website: https://thenewpress.org/contact-us.

Published in the United States by The New Press, New York, 2026
Distributed by Two Rivers Distribution

ISBN 978-1-62097-974-7 (hc)
ISBN 978-8-89385-003-1 (ebook)
CIP data is available

The New Press publishes books that promote and enrich public discussion and
understanding of the issues vital to our democracy and to a more equitable world.
These books are made possible by the enthusiasm of our readers; the support of a
committed group of donors, large and small; the collaboration of our many partners in
the independent media and the not-for-profit sector; booksellers, who often hand-sell
New Press books; librarians; and above all by our authors.

www.thenewpress.org

Composition by Bookbright Media
This book was set in Janson Text and Config Variable

Printed in the United States of America

10 9 8 7 6 5 4 3 2 1

To all those in need of healing and belonging through restorative justice.

*You never change things by fighting the existing reality.
To change something, build a new model that makes the
existing model obsolete.*

—Buckminster Fuller

*Restorative justice advocates dream of a day when justice is
fully restorative, but whether this is realistic is debatable,
at least in the immediate future. More attainable, perhaps,
is a time when restorative justice is the norm, while some
form of the legal or criminal justice system provides the
backup or alternative. Possible, perhaps, is a time when
all our approaches to justice will be restoratively oriented.
Society must have a system to sort out the "truth" as best it
can when people deny responsibility. Some cases are simply
too difficult or horrendous to be worked out by those with
a direct stake in the offense. We must have a process that
gives attention to those societal needs and obligations that go
beyond the ones held by the immediate stakeholders. We also
must not lose those qualities which the legal system at its best
represents: the rule of law, due process, a deep regard for
human rights, the orderly development of law.*

—Howard Zehr, *The Little Book of Restorative Justice*

Applied in schools, the principles of restorative justice provide adults and children with processes like the Circle process, for holding students (and adults) accountable for rule violations, such as fights and bullying. . . . But the Circle process and the principles of restorative justice offer more than this. If the Circle is used only to repair harm, then this simple yet profound communication process becomes associated with frustration, anger and shame. By contrast, if Circles are also used to build relationships and community, then, when you must use Circle to mend harms, the hard conversations can look like magic. As with most things the magic is in the practice. Clarity and reconciliation come as a result of practicing the Circle process.

—Nancy Riestenberg, *Circle in the Square:
Building Community and Repairing Harm in School*

Contents

RESTORATIVE JUSTICE UP CLOSE

Foreword

HOWARD ZEHR

A former faculty colleague of mine, a history professor, used to complain that what students most remembered from his lectures were the stories he told. He shouldn't have been surprised. Stories engage us, inspire us, and ultimately educate us. More than that, our lives are built on stories. Stories are how we form and share our identities. When bad or traumatic things happen to us, we often have to heal by reconstituting a new narrative about ourselves that incorporates what happened and how we responded. Storytelling is a form of metacognition: a fundamental "way of knowing" and being.

This is a book of stories emanating from the expanding field of restorative justice, one that I helped to found in the United States some fifty years ago. Longtime practitioner Sally Wolf solicited stories of cases from participants and facilitators in a wide variety of settings, all recounting how restorative justice circles and victim-offender conferences elicited healing, wholeness, and belonging. The stories offer hope for what can emerge from difficult and often seemingly intractable situations.

I was once involved in a documentary film about restorative justice that was translated into Spanish for South American audiences. I was later told that one of the translators knew of a local situation where harm had been done. He was so inspired and motivated by the film that, based on what he learned during the translation, he was able to facilitate a successful conference with the individuals. I don't necessarily recommend facilitating without some training, but it does demonstrate the potential of stories to empower people to change the way they interact with other community members to pursue justice.

Of course, not all restorative justice cases end perfectly, and this volume includes stories from practitioners who admit to mistakes in approach and reflect on their learnings. However, the primary purpose of this volume is not instructional, but instead illustrative. This powerful collection of stories does something similar to what the documentary film did for the translator: It expands our visions of what is possible and provides ideas about how restorative justice principles and practices might be applied in our own lives and workplaces.

Introduction

SALLY SWARTHOUT WOLF

I don't remember a lot about the year I spent in kindergarten. But I do remember my teacher, Miss Coffee. I remember nap time every day, when we had to lie down on the mats we had brought from home and rest. Miss Coffee would walk around the room and say in a very soft voice, "Everyone is quiet. There is not a sound in the room. Every bone is still." I remember wiggling my toes inside my shoes mischievously and thinking that they were the only thing moving in the entire room.

Years later when I was in junior high school, that memory came back to me during a dinner table conversation one night. I shared it with my family, thinking they would enjoy my story of rebellious toe wiggling. But instead, my dad said to me, "You're old enough now to say her name right. Her name was Mrs. McCarthy."

"What?! That can't be! Everybody called her Miss Coffee!" I looked at him in outraged disbelief. But he was right; her name *was* Mrs. McCarthy.

As an adult, I've often reflected on that experience, and how all of us can persist in a state of surety about a mistaken belief, and even in the belief that everyone we know believes it, too. How on Earth could we be wrong? In 2013, Alberto Brandolini, an Italian computer programmer, addressed the difficulty of debunking misinformation by observing that "The amount of energy needed to refute BS is an order of magnitude bigger than that needed to produce it."[1] While he was referring to the popularization of errant ideas through the internet and social media, the principle itself has likely been true since the beginning of humankind.

And so it is with the American criminal justice system and approaches to school discipline. In 1974, a sociologist named Robert Martinson conducted a study that suggested widespread shortcomings in programs intended to rehabilitate offenders in the justice system. His findings, which became known as the "Nothing Works" doctrine, significantly impacted criminal justice practices by shifting focus away from rehabilitation and toward punishment, becoming one of several causes of massively increased prison populations.[2]

Martinson eventually rescinded his finding that "nothing works" some years after his 1974 study, and yet retributive justice remains the principal approach to resolving cases of lawbreaking and harm. According to a 2018 study by the U.S. Department of Justice's Bureau of Justice Statistics, 66 percent of people incarcerated in 2008 had been rearrested within three years of their release; 82 percent would be rearrested within ten years.[3] And yet most justice officials and ordinary citizens believe fervently in punishment as the best way to maintain social order and deter future crime.

Setting aside the question of whether retributive justice makes us safer, a major flaw in this punitive ideology is that it often ignores the wishes of victims. Victims consistently express a preference for rehabilitation programs that would help prevent the person who hurt them from harming others. They often have questions about the "why?" of the offense and want their offender to understand the impact it wrought on them. Crime survivors often feel that the current justice system does not really care about their needs.

In a parallel phenomenon to mass incarceration, schools experienced a sharp increase in suspensions and expulsions after adopting "zero tolerance" discipline policies in the 1990s. By the 2010s, studies began to show that suspending kids doubled the chance of dropping out,[4] greased a path to the criminal justice system, and contributed to a climate of distrust and disconnection within schools.

Fortunately, momentum for an alternative approach to justice and student discipline has been building in the United States and other countries. In the late 1970s Howard Zehr, a Mennonite criminologist, founded the Victim Offender Reconciliation Program in Elkhart, Indiana. The program was based on principles that emphasized resolving conflicts and repairing harm through facilitated conversations between affected parties and their supporters. Zehr called this approach "Restorative Justice." Similar models developed in the latter part of the twentieth century in Australia, New Zealand, Europe, and Canada. While practices differed, the principles were the same, based in the worldview and mindset of Indigenous communities around the world, that people are profoundly relational, interconnected, and inherently good.

People embraced restorative justice as a better means of meeting the needs for healing and repair. Schools took up restorative practices, which helped to build community in the schools, while providing an alternative response to harm besides suspension.

Sharing stories can show how restorative justice works. Instead of focusing solely on the question of what laws or rules were disobeyed and "who did it," restorative justice asks a different set of questions. It asks, "Who was harmed? What has been the impact of that harm, and how can it and the breach in relationships be repaired?"

The offender[5] has an obligation to assist with restoring what has been damaged. Sometimes that can be as simple as restitution and a heartfelt apology; it can also involve working together with the person harmed to address the wrongdoing. However, that repair takes place with the participation of the person harmed. Affected community members provide support and accountability for the offender to make amends and support and care for the person harmed. All voices are welcome and heard. Rather than casting those who have broken rules out of the community, restorative practices draw them in. Studies find that, by doing so, people who participate in a restorative process are less likely to recidivate, and victim satisfaction is considerably higher than in regular justice processes.[6]

Several variations of restorative practices are used, depending on the context and circumstances. In criminal justice settings, the most common practices are family group conferencing (in cases involving youth), victim-offender mediation or dialogues (in cases involving adults), and community reparative boards. These practices can take place at all stages of the justice system, from accusation to sentencing.

However, the most common evidence-based practice is to convene participants in a circle together with a trained facilitator, with everyone committing to speaking only in turn and listening closely to what is being said. In classrooms, peacemaking circles are used to focus young students on building and maintaining positive relationships. Students are encouraged to take ownership of their actions, work together to repair harm, and find solutions to conflicts. Mutual respect is achieved through communication that builds trust and empathy. Entry and reentry circles are used when new students arrive and when suspended or expelled students return to school. Schools that have adopted restorative practices report lower rates of suspension and higher academic performance; students report a greater sense of belonging.[7]

In justice contexts, so-called "circles of support and account-ability" have a demonstrated capacity to enhance the safe reintegration of offenders into their communities.[8] By giving harmed parties a voice in the resolution of their cases, victims who participate in restorative conferences report a high rate of satisfaction and greater peace of mind than those who go through the regular justice process.[9]

Despite this evidence, restorative justice continues to encounter skepticism and challenge. The most common doubt one hears is whether restorative justice really holds people accountable or instead allows them to "get off" with a slap on the wrist, especially when the offense is serious. Others worry about retraumatizing victims by putting them in the same room with the person who harmed them.

I first encountered restorative practices when working as director of probation and court services in Ford County, Illinois. We used it in youth and eventually adult cases. I soon realized that the outcomes we were getting through restorative justice were far superior to the regular terms of probation and community service we'd been imposing, in both lower recidivism and higher participant satisfaction. As I began training others through an organization I co-founded along with others called Illinois Balanced and Restorative Justice, I found that sharing stories about some of my conferences was the best way to alleviate the concerns of skeptics. Sharing only statistics about victim satisfaction or lower recidivism rates just didn't resonate with people who were certain that wrongdoers need to be punished and victims separated and protected from them. I found telling stories made a huge difference in helping them to understand the power of restorative practices.

I searched for a volume that related stories of what actually transpires in a restorative justice session, but I could not find one. So

I set out to collect first-person accounts of restorative conferences and the difference they made to the parties involved. Because restorative conferences are trust-based processes that operate under a pledge of confidentiality, they are rarely videotaped and never transcribed. This required storytellers to get permission from participants, which was often a long and laborious process. This volume was very much an undertaking of love and belief that stories can help people build new mental models for what justice and conflict resolution look like.

In this book, I have included stories across a range of contexts and variations of practice. There are stories of restorative justice in K–12 schools, in youth crimes, in prison, and in the resolution of hate crimes. Many will be surprised to learn that restorative justice can be positively implemented in crimes as serious as homicide, and this book includes several of those cases as well. Most of the stories in this volume are related by restorative justice facilitators, but the book also includes stories told by victims, offenders, judges, and a police officer—all attesting to the "heart shift" that can occur when people share openly and honestly their pain, their motivation, their needs, and their mistakes, and together make a plan for repair. These are things that a regular justice process or punishment alone simply do not achieve.

My hope is that these stories will help you—or perhaps a skeptical colleague—understand the power of facilitated dialogue as a means to resolving conflict and harm, and why restorative justice is the best-kept secret in our country today. Long-held beliefs are worth reexamining, whether about something as small as the name of a long-ago kindergarten teacher or as big as what constitutes "justice."

Part One

Restorative Practices in Schools

1.

School Discipline and Bullying

Schools across the United States and Canada are taking up restorative justice as a superior means of resolving disciplinary issues over suspension and detention. As some of the stories in this chapter demonstrate, school administrators are also learning that the inquiry-based process of restorative justice engenders a level of trust that better elicits the underlying reasons for a student's misbehavior. This allows school staff to fashion appropriate interventions and supports for the student.

In school contexts, we often use the term "restorative practices" rather than restorative justice, because its principles are applicable to contexts well beyond discipline. For example, many teachers in K–12 schools are now convening "morning circles" with their students at the start of the day to check in and connect with one another, thereby fostering closer relationships and empathy within the classroom. Other schools are employing it to resolve tensions among school staff.

By modeling empathetic listening and collaboration, restorative practices are also teaching students important social and emotional skills: how to listen, how to regulate their behavior, and how to resolve conflicts on their own. Schools are also finding that by strengthening relationships between students, restorative practices reduce bullying (which, as the story from Will Bledsoe emphasizes, sometimes calls for a different protocol).

The Importance of Building Community

Nancy Michaels

About ten or twelve years ago I was associate director of the Mansfield Institute for Social Justice and Transformation at Roosevelt University in Chicago. We were researching the school-to-prison pipeline in Chicago schools. It was during this research that I first learned about restorative justice. I read everything I could get my hands on and began reaching out to learn from those in the Chicago and statewide restorative justice community.

Several months later at a block party in my neighborhood, I was introduced to a neighbor, Michael Beyer, who explained that he was beginning a new position in a few weeks as the principal of the Morrill Elementary Math and Science School. He shared his concern about the high rate of suspensions and expulsions he'd seen in the school's data and expressed interest in introducing "some kind of social justice programming" into the school. When we discussed the concept of restorative justice in schools, he was intrigued and wanted to know more. The school was in the Gage Park neighborhood of Chicago, with a predominantly Black student body and a smaller number of Latino students. Its high suspension rate was consistent with emerging research that showed that students of color are suspended and expelled disproportionally to white students.

On a Saturday in August, just before the start of the school year, we gathered in circle with the Morrill school staff and engaged in a daylong experiential introduction to restorative justice. We presented a three-year plan for a "whole school approach" to restorative justice. Together we created a "peace room" that the students helped to decorate. The peace room was painted with inspiring quotes on the walls, furnished with art supplies and floppy beanbag chairs, and became a safe space for proactive and responsive peacemaking circles.

The students loved the peace room, so much so that often we would have a line of them waiting to be in this welcoming space; we even had snacks hidden in drawers! Often, students would come to school on Monday having witnessed violence in their communities or other life challenges over the weekend. The peace room was a place to help students reflect, share emotions, and deal with those experiences. It was a space also to address harm as well as to hold what we referred to as "talking circles" to discuss just about anything: issues around race, culture, family, celebration, preparing for testing, grieving—just to name a few. The story I relate here was typical of many incidents that we were able to resolve through restorative justice.

One day, not long before summer break, a teacher at the school spied the shove and the punch from the corner of her eye on the playground. Before things got worse, she approached the boys, pulled them aside, and engaged in a "restorative chat" that prevented the incident from going any further. A restorative chat is a quick de-escalation approach to open up the lines of communication. It includes asking each participant a series of questions to explain what happened and what they were thinking/feeling at the time. For example: What happened? What were you thinking at the time? Who do you think was impacted? What do we need to do to make it right?

This teacher wrote up a restorative justice conflict circle referral form requesting that a peace circle take place to go deeper than the on-the-spot chat allowed. On the form, she provided a brief explanation of what had happened and sent it to the restorative justice team.

After reviewing the referral, we met with the two third-grade boys, Javon and Edward, individually in order to ensure both were agreeable to moving forward with a circle, as well as with a few of the students on the playground who had witnessed the incident. Then we gathered in the peace room. The circle centerpiece was full of coveted "talking pieces" such as family photos, small stuffed animals, and feathers that kids had brought from home throughout the year, along with some rocks that the younger students had painted for use in the peace room. The students began to file in, taking a seat in the beanbag chairs—some of them with nervous giggles, others somber, and still others with expressions of frustration, all of them rustling in their chairs.

I picked up the brass chimes from the center and clinked them together as a sign that the circle would begin. We read aloud the values that students and staff at Morrill Elementary had agreed to and posted on a large piece of newsprint paper taped to the wall: being honest, respecting the talking piece, and listening carefully. As a reminder, I asked, "Does everyone still agree with these values today?" We passed the talking piece around and all agreed. "Good, then, these will be our values for our circle today. Let's check in. Tell us how you're feeling today, and, if you could be a superhero, who would you be and why?" There were lots of one-word answers: Tired, hungry, I feel okay. . . . Most got into the superhero part.

I saw that we needed to share a bit more before moving on to the matter at hand. We picked another talking piece. How was your weekend and what is one thing you enjoyed doing? Most shared more in response to this question with answers like "I slept at my grandma's house"; "I played outside at the park"; "My mom took us shopping." When the talking piece got to Edward, he mumbled something undiscernible, turned his head to the side, and passed the talking piece to Alexis on his left.

I asked, "Edward, we couldn't make out what you said. Would you mind repeating it?" Alexis handed him back the piece, and Edward mumbled a bit louder, "I'm okay. It was my birthday," and dropped the talking piece on Alexis's lap. Most in the circle blurted out, "Happy birthday, Edward!" There were some high fives in the air. "Wow, it was your birthday!"

When the round concluded and I got the talking piece back, I said, "Okay, well, it sounds like we all had a nice weekend; mine was nice, too," and I shared a little about my weekend with my family.

We moved on to the focus of the circle. "We are here today because there was an incident on the playground this morning. Please share in your own words what happened this morning on the playground."

I passed the talking piece, and some of the students energetically shared what they saw, while others did so quietly, with heads down; still other students chose to pass. When it came to Javon, his face turned red, and he explained that Edward cut in front of him; then, when Javon pushed him out of the way, Edward socked him in the stomach.

When Edward got the piece he said, "Yeah, I punched him and . . ." He grumbled something. I asked him to repeat what he said, and he put his head down and dropped the talking piece on Alexis's lap. I asked her to send it my way. There was some chattering back and forth, and I used the brass chimes again to settle down the group.

"Okay, let's share a bit about how this made you feel." The talking piece went around. Several responded that they were angry, including Javon. Some said they thought there would be a fight, and others said they didn't know how they felt. When the talking piece made it to Edward, he mumbled something with his head down. I asked him again to speak up, and he blurted out, "You were wrong, Ms. Nancy; I didn't have a good weekend! My dad never came for my birthday."

I asked for the piece before responding, "I'm so sorry he never made it, and I'm sorry I jumped to conclusions and assumed your weekend was good because it was your birthday. Now I understand why you didn't have a good weekend. Is there anything else you want to share about how you felt?"

"No."

"Thank you for sharing with us, Edward," I said. I passed the piece and asked that we all continue sharing how we were feeling now. At this point, Javon was waving his hand back and forth and finally asked if he could speak. I sent the talking piece his way. He took it, looked across the circle at Edward, and said, "Man, I haven't seen my dad for years, so I know how you must have felt."

The room was still. Edward lifted his head up for the first time in the circle. Javon passed the piece to Matt sitting to his left, who said, "Sorry that your dads didn't come to your birthdays, Edward and Javon." Others got the piece and shared similar sentiments. The circle had moved in another direction, and it was clear that Edward and Javon had something in common now, and their peers in the circle knew them each more intimately.

We continued to our discussion about how certain feelings can cause us to take out our anger and hurt on others in ways that can cause harm and are not okay. We then discussed what might be better ways of handling sadness or anger. But the most impactful outcome of the circle was the empathy that had surfaced, and the relationships that were built. Empathy, understanding, being connected and in right relationship results in less harm and increased support for one another as well as that all-important sense of belonging.

Our work at Morrill to achieve a "whole school approach" to restorative justice—practiced every day in multiple ways—became apparent by the end of the second year. The preventive work of regular morning check-ins and talking circles was taking place, teachers and staff were using restorative language, and almost everyone was trained in restorative justice approaches. The outcomes included a reduction in suspensions and expulsions, an increased sense of connectedness between students and staff, an increase in family involvement, and an overall culture of caring.

Those Affected Will Always Know Best

Kathy Rockefeller

I was just learning about restorative justice through my work with incar-cerated people preparing to reenter the community. Each year, many of them indicated that their experience with getting in trouble "all started with a middle school suspension." Research confirming the school-to-prison pipeline—the link between the use of harsh school discipline that removes children from school, and an exponentially increased likelihood of involve-ment in the criminal justice system—was just emerging. I realized that I was working with the people most affected by this form of school discipline. I shifted my professional focus to restorative practices in schools, aimed at keeping youth from entering the pipeline altogether.

Around that time, an "alternative" school (a school for students who exhaust their home school's discipline ladder) invited me to help brain-storm next steps around a student conflict impacting their school com-munity. Every one of the approximately twenty girls in the high school program was involved in repeated fighting. Standard exclusionary conse-quences (such as in-school or out-of-school suspensions) were not working. In the room with these school leaders—some of the most talented educators I have ever met—I heard their disheartening plan: Invite all the girls and their parents to a meeting together and deliver a no-nonsense mes-sage about what was at stake—more extreme punishment—if the girls kept fighting.

I was curious: Hadn't they already been told what was at stake? What would be different? Tentatively, I suggested circle seating (rather than rows of chairs with staff in front) and, at least to start, no parents. My experience was that, given the right setting, students are better at resolv-ing their own conflict than the adults around them, no matter how well-intentioned and caring. I could tell there were strong doubts in the room,

but, in their sheer desperation and exhaustion, the educators agreed to
allow me to lead the girls in a responsive circle and give them the chance
to resolve their own conflict.

When the girls arrived, they sat in the empty chairs, clearly angry
that they could not sit in their normal groups. Those "groups" were
easy to spot, as were their respective leaders. There were three distinct cliques, wearing distinct colors and making eye contact with
their leader before sitting or answering questions. We formed a
circle in the cafeteria with an equal number of school staff and students. It was a huge circle, and I worried about people being able to
hear each other in that cavernous space. We had the adults arrive
first and sit with an empty chair between them.

As the circle keeper, I quickly introduced myself and my talking
piece and reviewed basic circle guidelines. The tension was palpable, and I remember sensing that we needed to get the conversation started before someone's side-eye sparked a fight. I shared
the safety plan: "If you feel you are going to lose control against
someone in this circle, please leave the circle with the adult to your
right, drain off, and return when you are ready to continue. We will
continue the conversation, and you can rejoin when you are ready."
Giving permission to take breaks communicated that this process
would be different—that their need for time and space would be
honored without question or examination. Stating that we would
continue in their absence communicated that one individual would
not be permitted to hijack the process for everyone else. It also created motivation to return quickly; students in conflict do not like
to miss anything that might be said against them.

We began with Restorative Question No. 1: "What is happening between you?" As they passed the talking piece, the silence was

deafening. I repeated the question and sent the talking piece around again, a mild panic creeping up my neck. Some adults answered this time, but still no students. After three rounds (which felt like an eternity), one of the young women suddenly stood, pointed the talking piece at a girl across the circle, and screamed: "I'll tell you what's going on! You want to fight me, and I am telling you right now, my address is _____!" This caused an anxious flurry of unrest, and the adult to her right stood and invited the student to step out for a few minutes with her, which she did. The talking piece kept moving.

That outburst opened the floodgates. The girls all participated eagerly as their turns arrived. There were many accusations, insults, and emotions. Students replied, often with high volume and salty language, without correction by the staff in the room. The process was for them to use as they needed. There were more exits of students with their assigned adults, and it was affirming to watch them choose to use that resource. Each time a student stepped out, I encouraged everyone to make the circle smaller and continue the conversation. I trusted the adults who left with the students were calming them and helping them process the situation. At least once, the school resource officer was consulted because of a student's escalation, and that student did not return to the circle.

I had very little actual experience facilitating conflict circles at the time, and I wondered if it would work. At times, fewer than half of us remained in the circle. Thankfully, there were as many reentries into the circle as there were exits. Each time, the participants widened the circle again to accommodate the return without fanfare, and we continued. The whole experience felt messy and uncomfortable to me. And yet the girls continued to participate and respect the process. It was clear they had never heard each other's perspective before, and they wanted to hear and be heard. It also became clear that one of the girls was mostly neutral and respected by all—a "Switzerland," if you will.

After almost two hours, their answers to Restorative Question No. 1 ("What is happening between you?") were still going strong. As the facilitator, I knew we were reaching the limit of time that people can handle a high-level conflict circle. Then I was abruptly informed that lunch started in ten minutes, so we needed to wrap it up. *Ugh!* Emotions were all over the place and there was no resolution in sight. If they did not sense a resolution was possible, what might happen when the circle stopped? Was it safe to allow them to leave the cafeteria and the structure of the adult-supported circle?

When I regained the talking piece, I said: "We will continue this circle tomorrow. It is up to each of you whether you want to participate and there is no penalty for choosing not to participate. If you choose to participate, however, you will begin creating a peaceful way forward for yourselves. You know what will work for you better than any of us adults, and we want you to have the chance to create the solution for yourselves. I am sending the talking piece around for one final question: 'Are you in or out tomorrow?'" Every single girl said she was "in."

When we met the following day, the mood was palpably different, which I have since found is often true when students have a night to process. When asked who was affected by the girls' actions, the adults—to a person—were vulnerable and shared how defeated this situation had made them feel. This was a group of dedicated educators who had worked to build strong relationships with these students, and yet they felt they'd failed them. Upon hearing this, the students began spontaneously addressing specific adults when it was their turn with the talking piece, often apologizing and owning their contributions to the situation. They insisted they did not consider the adults failures and were sorry their actions made them feel that way.

By the time we got to Restorative Question No. 5 ("What can *you* do to make things better?"), the answers were insightful and fantastic. The girls felt that part of the problem was they did not know each other, which made it easier to view their classmates as enemies. This sparked the adults to realize what *they* could do to make things better: coordinate events to help the girls get to know each other. The educators proceeded to describe, specifically, what they would do to help create some fun events. When one student fondly remembered making stress balls with a staff member, that staff member offered to plan for all the girls to make stress balls together. When a student mentioned how a picnic had once helped students meet each other, a different staff person said she'd plan a new picnic, and several other adults chimed in with offers to lead the activities, reserve space, and arrange food. When a student remembered a time a local department store hosted a fashion show for the students, an adult volunteered to reach out to the store again, and the principal promised to approve it if the girls worked to earn it.

Everyone was getting excited and there was a lot of relieved laughter among the girls and the adults. You could feel the tension dissipate and the camaraderie bloom. The students could not believe these adults were happier arranging positive things for them than suspending and disciplining them! It was wonderful to see the girls craft their own relationship building, and a true honor to witness the spark reappear in the educators' eyes.

The students, meanwhile, pledged to do things like go directly to their classmates before believing what someone said about them, and to go to a particular staff person to request a circle if things began bubbling up again. The girl who was "Switzerland" offered to be available to her classmates who needed to privately check if specific rumors were true. The students offered to remind their friends about the new agreements when they were getting heated and tempted to fight. In addition to more community-building activities and events—things that had been abandoned in the name of "safety" because of feuds—the girls were building a plan for peace in their own school community. The adults followed the students' lead and built supports around the girls' plan so that it was realistic in the school setting.

For me, this experience was life changing. I witnessed and felt the power of a restorative circle in a seemingly hopeless situation. I felt the sincere acknowledgment and acceptance of responsibility by students and saw them empowered to allow creativity and collaboration replace the hatred and threats of just the day before. I was deeply moved and forever convinced of the promise of restorative practices to create peaceful learning environments and decrease the number of students entering the school-to-prison pipeline.

Listening to our children participate in a structured and safe process, surrounded by caring and committed adults, taught me that students are fully capable of resolving their own conflicts. Adults can approach student conflicts as fellow members of the school community, with teaching hearts, using processes designed to help students feel safe to participate. Students can practice conflict resolution skills that fit their own lives and be better equipped to contribute to their communities as adults. The students' solutions, and the adults' support of those solutions, were infinitely better and more appropriate than what we typically offer in schools, and the process gave them the buy-in to make their solutions a reality.

I returned for their first community-building event a week or so later. It was a gathering in that same cafeteria with stations at which the girls could do various fun activities together, including making stress balls! The young women, who were not safe to be together a week before, were having a great time moving from station to station and freely co-mingling with girls in the other groups.

I had typed up all their circle agreements, and one station allowed them to sign their name to it. They all signed. None of the girls who participated was suspended for fighting for the remainder of that school year, and the morale of the staff—so many of whom had participated in the solution—soared. The school quickly adopted restorative practices and became a district model. Yes, the circle had felt messy and uncomfortable at first, but the status quo at that time was also messy and uncomfortable, and at times dangerous. Both the students and staff brought their best selves to the circle, and the whole community contributed to heal itself.

This circle taught me a few things. I no longer plan circles that large in a school setting, especially when there has been physical harm. Despite the good outcome, I believe the risk was too high, and if it weren't for the extraordinarily close relationships that had already been fostered between students and staff at that school, it might have had a different result. That does not mean I shy away from using restorative practices with large, complex student conflicts. Instead, I am now more likely to use a series of smaller, carefully planned and prepped circles. Before deciding how many circles and which students to include in each, I conduct individual precircle interviews with all potential participants using a protocol I designed to build trust, decrease anxiety, and gain information. After all interviews are complete, I use the information I have gained to map out various combinations of students, in various possible circles. Then I make a judgment about what is the best place to start. Sometimes, I start with the two who are at the very center of the conflict. Other times, it feels safer to start with students who are on the perimeter but who may hold some sway with those at the center. Ultimately, this allows students to loosen the knot of their own conflict as the circles unfold. Once loosened, the conflict often resolves itself quickly, and sometimes further circles are not even needed.

Had I used this precircle interview protocol with the participants in this story, I believe we could have finished the larger circle in one sitting, with less stress for everyone involved. The overnight break between the two circles would still have helped shift the mood, but that shift could likely have occurred earlier, between the precircle interviews and the circle itself. Now that I have a better understanding of trauma, I also believe precircle interviews would have increased the psychological safety of the circle participants by allowing them to hear about the circle process and decrease the uncertainty and anxiety of a new process for them. I share these learnings whenever I train and always feel humble thanks to that first group of girls who provided so much insight.

The biggest lesson for me, though, is that when you offer an authentic circle process, and calmly sit with the participants as they navigate their own conflict, those affected are always in the best position to create solutions that work for them and will rise to the challenge.

Getting to the Real Issues: Avoiding Suspensions with Restorative Circles

Sandra Pavelka, PhD

The concept of restorative justice was first introduced to me in 1994 when I was directing a youth policy center at Nova Southeastern University Law Center, administering the National Detention Alternative Initiative, which sought to reduce youth incarceration. Restorative justice was new to me and to the staff in the juvenile justice system with whom I interacted. But I knew that those systems officials wanted to see changes in the youth legal system that had become overly punitive in nature. Restorative justice offered us an alternative and a much-needed paradigm shift.

But over time, I came to believe that in order to make a significant and lasting impact, we needed restorative justice in educational settings, where many young people begin to go offtrack and are pushed out of school and into the criminal justice system. I turned my attention to providing training and technical assistance on restorative strategies in districts in my home state of Florida.

One case that had a lasting impression on me involved a fourth-grade girl at an elementary school in a coastal community of Florida. Maria was in jeopardy of being suspended from school due to her habitual tardiness and truancy, and she was referred to a restorative circle with the objective of developing a plan for improvement. The circle was held in an empty classroom after school in order to avoid further loss of instructional time for Maria. Eight chairs were placed in a circle, with a dozen talking pieces laid upon a centerpiece. The talking pieces had all been made by students in art class for use during restorative circles. In addition to Maria, participants included the circle keeper and facilitator, Miss Anne;

Maria's fourth-grade teacher, Ms. Nash; the assistant principal for discipline, Mr. Wells; the school counselor, Ms. Jenkins; the school resource officer, Officer Diggs; and a student representative named Jack. I attended as a neutral observer. Miss Anne welcomed all the participants to the circle and asked Maria to choose a talking piece. She then reviewed the circle norms with all of the participants:

- Listening well, to understand the speaker's perspective.
- Confidentiality, to protect the privacy of each person in the circle.
- Respect, so that the circle is a safe place to express thoughts and emotions.
- Honesty, to build trust with ourselves and others.
- Equality, such that each participant has a chance to help create the restorative circle agreement.

After everyone agreed to the circle norms, Miss Anne read an opening quote from *Oh, the Places You'll Go* by Dr. Seuss: "You have brains in your head. / You have feet in your shoes. / You can steer yourself any direction you choose. / You're on your own. / And you know what you know. / And YOU are the one who'll decide where to go. . . ." Mr. Wells, the assistant principal for discipline, reviewed the reason for the circle: Although Maria had never misbehaved in school, she had been habitually tardy and had numerous unexcused absences. She was at risk of being suspended from school.

Mr. Wells passed the talking piece to Maria, who immediately began crying. She was a soft-spoken, introverted young girl who didn't talk much in school. Maria said she didn't mean to be late and didn't want to miss school; she loved school and loved her friends. Maria said she was sorry over and over again.

Miss Anne gently asked Maria why she had been late for school so many times. Grasping the talking piece, Maria kept quiet, sobbing softly, before sharing that her mother was a maid at a beach hotel and had to leave home at 5 a.m. every morning in order to get to work on time. Also, Maria had two younger sisters—one six years old and one seven years old. As the oldest sibling, Maria was responsible for waking her sisters up in the morning, getting them ready for school, preparing breakfast for them, and then walking them to school. Because of her responsibilities, Maria was unable to get to school on time. If one of her siblings was ill, Maria stayed home from school and took care of her. She continued to sob as she told her story, but we could also sense her relief in confessing the truth of her situation, as if a weight were being lifted from her shoulders.

Miss Anne asked Maria to pass the talking piece to Ms. Nash, her fourth-grade teacher. Ms. Nash shared that Maria was a kind and friendly student, but also that when she entered the classroom late, it disrupted her instruction to the other students in the classroom. She had noticed that Maria looked tired many mornings and seemed overwhelmed at times. She was once an A student, but her grades were slipping to C's and D's, and she was in jeopardy of receiving an F in math. Ms. Nash also shared that Maria was having difficulty seeing the whiteboard in class, and that her clothes and shoes were worn. With evident care in her voice, Ms. Nash said she would provide resources to help Maria in any way she needed.

Ms. Jenkins, the school counselor, took the talking piece next. She shared that Maria had occasionally come to talk with her, expressing her sadness and concern about her mother and her sisters, but never sharing too much information with her. Ms. Jenkins expressed deep concern with what she was now hearing about Maria's situation.

Officer Diggs, the school resource officer, confirmed that Maria was a well-behaved student and never received any referrals for misbehaving or acting out. He had often seen Maria walking to school late and alone.

Miss Anne turned the conversation to how we might address the issues and work on a circle agreement. The talking piece was passed to Assistant Principal Wells, who shared that he was a member of the Lions Club, a local community organization that could provide financial assistance for vision care. He could speak to them about sponsoring Maria for an eye exam and glasses at the local optometrist.

Ms. Nash agreed to set up tutoring sessions in the subject areas Maria was struggling with, and expressed confidence that Maria would bring her grades up in due time. The talking piece was passed again to Ms. Jenkins, the school counselor, who shared that Maria would be welcome to look through the school's donation box of clothes and shoes and have her pick of what she would like. Ms. Jenkins also offered to see Maria on a weekly basis, and more often if needed.

Officer Diggs, the school resource officer, mentioned that there are parents who carpool and said he would reach out to several who live near Maria and ask if they would be able to drive her and her younger sisters to and from school.

The talking piece was then passed to Jack, the fifth eighth-grade student representative. Jack was a member of the National Junior Honor Society and volunteered to tutor Maria in math and science, and to be supportive if she ever needed to talk. He also reiterated that he would keep the conversation in the circle confidential. Jack passed the talking piece to Maria.

Maria was overwhelmed with emotion. She shared that she had been nervous and didn't know what would happen in the circle. Thanking everyone for their support and assistance, Maria said she would make things right, improve her grades, come to school on time, and make everyone in the circle proud of her. Maria said that she wanted to go to college one day and that the circle inspired her. Maria passed the talking piece to Miss Anne.

As the circle keeper and facilitator, Miss Anne reviewed the circle agreement and read it aloud for the circle participants to hear: Maria would attend school and be on time, a carpool would be coordinated to transport her to and from school, clothes and shoes would be available for her at the school counselor's office, tutors would be provided in the applicable subject areas, and the Lions Club would provide vision care and eyeglasses, if needed. She would be monitored until the end of the school year. Maria agreed with all of the terms of the agreement, as did all of the participants. Miss Anne printed it out and passed it around the circle for everyone to sign. Maria's mother was notified of the process and results. She shared her appreciation with the school.

Miss Anne thanked those in the circle for their participation and requested a moment of silent reflection. The talking piece then went around the circle one last time, with each person sharing one word that summed up their feeling in that moment. The words shared included "delighted, hopeful, inspired, elated, pleased, grateful, blessed"—and finally, from Maria, "thankful."

The Bully Inside Me

Will Bledsoe, PhD

Roughly a year before I began a doctoral program in communication at the University of Colorado in Boulder, two teenagers at Columbine High School shot and killed twelve classmates and a teacher, less than thirty miles from where I lived. When I heard that the killings might have been an act of revenge for bullying, I felt compelled to do something, as someone who had been bullied as a child. I understood on a visceral level how the feeling of humiliation can morph into a toxic desire for revenge.

As I searched for a focus for my dissertation, I reached out to Dr. Beverly Title, who had built a nationally recognized bully-proofing program for middle schools. She suggested I look into restorative justice, which, back then in 2000, was a relatively unknown form of peacemaking grounded in the ceremonial practices of the Diné people and other tribal communities. After participating in my first restorative circle, I realized that I had found a justice I had been unconsciously longing for on a personal level for my entire life. Restorative justice became the topic of my dissertation, and I have worked ever since in the field as a facilitator, trainer, program developer, and author of The Restorative Way: Harnessing the Power of Restorative Communication to Mend Relationships, Heal Trauma, and Reclaim Civility One Conversation at a Time *(2024).*

Bullying is the repeated use of threat, violence, or social exclusion in order to intimidate, belittle, demean, and dominate another person for the purpose of increasing the offender's perceived status and/or self-gratification. In my experience, restorative justice has much to offer in addressing bullying in schools, workplaces, and other contexts. However, applying restorative justice in this context requires specific protocols, because bullying is not merely a conflict; it is an act of relational terrorism

*that is fundamentally about power, and often masks shame in the offender
and elicits shame in victims.*

David was a twenty-one-year-old college student who was referred
to the university restorative justice program where I work. He had
started a fight at a party when another young man insulted him. A
friend of the man who had issued the insult jumped to the man's
defense, and the two proceeded to beat David severely. Other students intervened and told the two men to leave, which they did. No
one at the party knew them; they were party crashers.

When the police showed up, David ran. After they caught and
apprehended him, David tried to fight them, too. In the fight with
the two party crashers, he suffered a broken jaw, the loss of two
front teeth, a broken foot, a skull fracture, a concussion, and was
hospitalized for several weeks. After an investigation, the police
charged him with misdemeanor assault, brawling, and resisting
arrest. David was also in danger of being suspended by the university. The two men with whom he fought were never identified
or located.

When I met with David, he explained what he remembered
of that event. "My memory of the evening is not too clear. I
was drunk."

I took a deep breath and replied, "David, I'm sorry this happened
to you."

"Yeah, but I started the fight. They were defending themselves,"
he said.

"I understand that, and we'll talk about why you started the fight
in a moment. It's good that you are admitting to what you did, but,
David, there is no excuse for the damage these two assailants did to
you. They could've killed you."

He thought for a moment, then agreed with me. "Yeah. I thought about that when I was in the hospital." He then asked me, "Have you ever been beaten up?"

"Yes," I said. "I'll share my experience with you a bit later, but right now, I want to focus on your experience. Do you think you would've reacted differently if you weren't drunk?" I asked.

"To be honest, no. I'm sure the booze figured in, but I would've done the same thing, reacted the same way if I wasn't drunk," he said.

"Thanks for your honesty," I said. "Have you done this before?" I asked.

David thought for a moment. "Mr. Bledsoe, look at me. I'm short and I'm skinny. I'm an easy target."

"Were you bullied in high school?" I asked.

"Relentlessly. I learned to start the fight." When I asked him why, he said, "I felt like I needed to prove myself. Because I was always the 'small guy who got picked on,' I learned to pick fights with bigger guys immediately." He then added, "I usually lost."

"Like what happened here," I added.

"Yeah. Exactly what happened here," he said.

I was struck by how insightful this young man was about his defense mechanisms to bullying and was flooded by a tremendous feeling of compassion and admiration. I understood it. I'd been in his shoes. I shifted our conversation to asking who he felt was impacted by the fight. I had given him a questionnaire with the standard restorative justice questions before our meeting, and I could tell that he had given this one considerable thought in advance.

"My parents, the officers, and the university. My parents had to deal with my injuries and associated expenses, the officers had to take me to the emergency room, and the woman at the party was exposed to the violence. And I guess reports of fights like this one might deter parents from thinking this is a safe campus."

It surprised me that he had failed to mention that of all the people who were affected that night, he was the one who had suffered the most. I decided then to share a piece of my own history growing up in a pretty tough neighborhood.

As a kid, I endured repeated and often violent bullying. I wasn't just "picked on." Other boys (and girls) taunted me; called me names; made fun of the way I looked, talked, and walked; spread vicious rumors about me; threatened, hit, kicked, and beat me. Bullying paralyzed me psychologically and emotionally. I just instinctively froze with terror. I couldn't understand why other kids hated me so much. I was convinced that I was inherently bad, not likeable, not worthy. In sixth grade, I developed a bad stutter. Couldn't get the words out. Inevitably, it fueled further bullying. I couldn't make myself small enough.

When I graduated from high school, I thought that my ordeal was over, but I was wrong. All those incidents, all those times of being bullied, punched in the face, kicked, spit on, hit by rocks, taunted, teased, threatened, chased, and excluded had scarred me. The bully was now inside of me—a wound that poisoned my self-esteem, filled me with shame and rage, infected my relationships and degraded my physical health.

I told David, "I know what it's like to get beat up and feel humiliated. I always thought that because I was afraid and couldn't stand up to the bullies, I was a coward. In my late teens and early twenties, much like you, I started fights, trying to reconcile being bullied as a kid. But I was the only one telling myself that I was a coward. Getting help with that lie was part of my healing."

I could tell that what I said had moved him because he looked down and said, "Yeah. You get it."

"Yeah. I get it." I continued. "What I finally realized, after many years, was that I was essentially bullying myself. I was beating myself up. By this I mean that I was punishing myself with a false core belief that there was something fundamentally wrong with me for feeling afraid and not standing up for myself physically. I was still blaming myself. The second thing I realized was that the bullying didn't happen because of something wrong with me, but because of something wrong in our society that equates 'manhood' with being tough, aggressive, domineering, insensitive, and uncaring about others."

"Boys will be boys," he said.

"Right. As if bullying others is a natural and normal part of being a boy," I added.

I turned the conversation to the question of repair: "To whom do you think you need to make amends?" Referring to his answer on the preconference questionnaire he'd filled out, I said, "I don't think you need to apologize to the police or your parents unless it will make you feel better. I think you need to apologize to yourself. David, you were the one who was most impacted by what happened. Listening to you and your experience of being bullied, I have to ask: Can you see the connection? Can you forgive yourself? What would that look like for you?"

David's eyes watered, but he remained silent.

I explained the process of meeting with others in a circle to discuss what had happened and to put a plan in place to repair the damage, and I told David I was going to choose people who could offer support. I said, "We're going to hold bullying accountable. One way to do that is to invite people to participate in your circle who have been bullied." I said, "Being bullied leaves us feeling alone. The way out of that loneliness is to realize that others have had the same experience."

"So, I'm not going to meet with others who witnessed that night?" he asked.

"That's a great question. No. First, it would be almost impossible to find other students who were there that night, much less the two men who beat you up. Second and more important, it's your story—your experience of bullying—that others need to hear. So, in a sense, you sharing your story of what happened that night, and what happened to you in high school and how you attempted to cope with that, will help others heal. They'll identify with you. If you ask me, you have the opportunity to restore a sense of justice for others by destigmatizing bullying. We can make that a part of your restorative contract for the courts."

Although I didn't go into detail with David, my twenty-four years of practice has taught me that it's important that facilitators working in a context of bullying take a trauma-informed approach in order to understand how this experience impacts a person's nervous system, brain chemistry, and functioning. Initially calling a circle between the offender and a victim risks retraumatizing the survivor. Addressing bullying in a restorative way requires equal parts accountability and support, and I have found this is often better accomplished in two separate circles.[10]

Because bullying is isolating, what victims first need to experience is their community embracing and protecting them in a stance of support. The *support circle*, which is what we were going to conduct for David, creates a safe space for survivors to explain what happened, express how they feel, how it impacted them, and to experience collective support and protection—without the offender being in the circle. In David's case, the real offenders were the bullies from his past. The two young men who beat David mercilessly were also offenders. Yes, David threw the first punch and would need to take responsibility for that, but that in no way justified their response, which was out of all proportion.

I made the decision to conduct a support circle as opposed to a typical restorative justice conference circle that would focus only on his charges. My hope was that David would know that the harm *to him* was being taken seriously, that he matters, and that the community will hold the aggressors accountable even if they are not there. The message a support circle gives the survivor, by contrast, is, "This didn't happen because of you, but because of the thinking and behavior of the other person—and we won't tolerate this."

An *accountability circle* is conducted with the offender, without the survivor present, in order to directly hold offenders accountable for their behavior. Participants from the community who attend the circle need to express two things: First, that this behavior impacted not only the other person, but *all of us*. Second, that such behavior will not be tolerated in our community. However, the offender—as a human being—is not condemned or shamed. Instead, the underlying thinking, reasons, and motivations for the bullying should be explored and addressed both in the discussion and in the reparative agreement. Whether an additional group circle including both parties should be held requires careful consideration by the facilitation team.

Of course, in David's case no one had been able to identify the two men who picked on him and then beat him up. But I had an idea for how we might address accountability when David asked, "What about the cops? Will they be there?"

"No," I said. "But one thing you might think about doing, which we can also include in your reparative contract with us, is to interview a couple of cops about their own experience of being bullied. I think you'd be surprised about how prevalent this is and how it doesn't matter what profession you choose. I see that you're an anthropology major with a minor in math. Maybe this could produce a powerful term paper?"

"Really? I could do that as part of my reparative contract?" he asked.

"Absolutely," I said.

David's eventual support circle was powerful. I enlisted about ten other people, including a trauma therapist who was a Vietnam vet. After thanking everyone for coming, and in accordance with the basic restorative conference script, I asked David to tell us what happened.

"I was at a party talking to a girl I had just met when this guy came up to us and said to her, 'You could do better than this scrawny weed.' When he said this, I punched him in the face. When I did this, he and one of his friends started to beat me up. They pushed me to the ground. The guy I punched jumped on my chest and started pummeling me in the face with his fists. His friend started kicking me really hard in the side and when I tried to roll over and escape, he started kicking me in the back and stomping me on the head. He was wearing boots. When other students saw this, they intervened and told the two guys to leave. I don't remember too much after that, but I remember the police came. I was still lying on the ground. When I saw them looking down at me, I got up and started to run away from them. I thought they were the two guys who were beating me. When the police caught me, one of them said, 'We need to get you to the hospital.' A few days later, the police officers came to the hospital and charged me with misdemeanor assault, brawling, and resisting arrest. When I went before the judge, I pled guilty. The judge referred me to this program before sentencing."

I was struck by David's detached, unemotional demeanor in recounting his story. It was as if he were telling a story about something that happened to someone else and not him. But as detached as he may have appeared, the facial expressions and body language of others in our circle told a different story. They were clearly moved. One of the members gasped and muttered, "Dear God."

I decided to skip the question about who was impacted and instead asked David to tell us about his injuries. "How did these two males hurt you physically, David? You mentioned to me that you were in the hospital for several weeks."

Again, he was very matter-of-fact. "They broke my jaw and knocked two of my front teeth out. They fractured my skull. I had a concussion and a broken foot. I think they broke my foot when they were stomping on me."

I let the heaviness of the imagery of his injuries settle. Silence is a powerful and often necessary component of a restorative discussion. After a moment, I asked David, "How did your parents respond to what happened to you? Did they come see you when you were in the hospital?"

"My mom came. My dad had to work."

"How did they respond?" I asked.

"Like I told you, they pretty much told me it was my fault and that's what happens when you start a fight."

The Vietnam vet who was a trauma specialist asked, "Can I interject here?"

"Yes," I said.

"David, it sounds like your parents were blaming you for what happened, that somehow you deserved what these two men did to you. Does that make sense?"

David thought for a moment. "Maybe. But I did start the fight and if I wouldn't have thrown that first punch, none of this would've happened."

The veteran continued, "I understand that. But it seems to me that you were setting a boundary with this guy who was demeaning you. You were sticking up for yourself. That speaks highly of your own self-respect. You chose to smack the guy. There were other ways you might've handled it, which I hope we can help you discover, but it seems to me you just reacted. If you want my opinion, punching that guy, however unwise, in no way justifies what they did to you."

"Totally agree," said another member of our circle. This was the expression of empathy for David I was hoping for. Another member asked, "Did the cops ever catch the guys who did this?"

"No. They weren't students. They were party crashers," he said. "No one knew who they were."

Another member, a man in his late twenties, added, "Yet you're the one who's being charged with assault. I'm sorry, but that seems completely unfair."

"Well," I said, "that's why the courts are giving us the opportunity to restore fairness. In my experience, if this conference with David is constructive, the judge who referred David's case to us is giving us the opportunity to help him. I want to hear from others in our circle. How did David's story and the injuries he experienced impact you? What came up for you?"

Our transgender person, Amber, spoke first. "When I was in high school and just coming to terms with my identity, I was ridiculed. People called me names. One time, after a dance, three guys beat me up. They punched me and kicked me. Other students looked on and were laughing. I told my mom and dad what happened. I told the vice principal what happened. None of them supported me. They blamed it on my 'alternative lifestyle.' The message I got was, 'This wouldn't have happened if you weren't so weird.' David, your story is my story."

Another circle member, a male also in his late twenties, shared next. "I understand the reactive impulse to start the fight. I did the same thing so many times, and I was always the guy who got accused of being 'out of my mind.' Nobody asked me, 'What happened to you? Why did you do what you did?' Bullying sucks. The bullies are never held accountable."

A woman also in her late twenties spoke up. "Why were you charged with assault and the other guys weren't caught? This is messed up. You're here because you're taking responsibility, but where is the justice for you?"

I let these statements percolate. I could see they had an effect on David because he looked down at the old worn carpet in front of us. I asked him, "David, what is it like to hear this?"

David responded, "I really appreciate your understanding." Addressing Amber, David said, "I'm sorry you got beat up for being who you are. I also appreciate all of your understanding of why I threw the first punch." And to the other young woman he said, "[About] your question, 'Where's the justice for me in this?' I don't know."

I steered us back on course. "That's what we're here to figure out. I trust we will." Referring to the veteran, I said, "I want to return to something you just said. You mentioned the word 'react.' Do you mean that we're re-acting out a previous scenario, story, or script?"

"That's exactly what I meant. It's a type of PTSD. When we experience a situation where our physical safety is threatened, like what happens in bullying, our threat response mechanisms get activated. We click into our primal survival brain. But that experience becomes a memory so ingrained that any time we feel threatened, real or imagined, we're back in that original threatening moment. I don't want to turn this into a therapy session, David, but did this guy's comments about you remind you of previous experiences?"

Without hesitation, David responded, "Yeah."

"So is it safe to say that you had just had enough?" the vet asked.

Again, without hesitation, David replied, "Yeah."

"Are you interested in disarming that trigger?" the vet asked. "Because, in my opinion, 'justice for you' would look like helping you to not get hooked when men are acting like assholes."

David responded, "Yeah. I'm really tired of this."

"I had to disarm my own PTSD triggers after coming back from the war," the veteran went on. "I had to 'reprogram' my fundamental reaction to sounds. I wasn't in the war anymore, but the war was inside of me and destroying my well-being."

"You get it," said David.

"Yeah, I get it," said the vet.

I moved us forward. "We need to talk about repair. What needs to be repaired here? How can we help David resolve his charges with the court but also find a way to meet David's needs?"

I asked David, "What do you think needs to be repaired?"

"I don't know, Mr. Bledsoe. I just want to do whatever I need to do to please the judge," he said. "I'm facing suspension from the university. It's like I'm under the rule of two different systems. I made a mistake. I shouldn't have started the fight. I admit that. What can I do?"

"I hear you. Maybe there's a way we can create a plan of repair that would meet both your needs and what the indirectly impacted 'community' might need," I said. "What I know is that both the court and the university's judicial affairs office are most concerned about making sure that a person is held accountable and keeping this from happening again. They're looking for change."

"I think you're under three systems, David," said the veteran. "The courts, the university, and your family system. Seems to me you deserve the most repair."

Amber asked, "Doesn't it make sense that if David repairs the damage done to him, the community benefits?"

I was hoping someone in our circle would ask this. I asked, "How can David address the harm done to him?"

"Healing from both what was done to him in high school but also this violent assault," said Amber.

Another participant stated, "I'm concerned about your parents, David. I'm concerned that they blamed you."

I added, "I want to remind us that we create the reparative plan working with David. Typically, the court requires some type of community service. I think if we help David find the resources to help him heal, that can suffice for service to the community. David, how does that sound to you?"

David replied, "You also said I could produce some type of essay or project for my anthropology class. Is that possible?"

"Yes," I said.

The veteran spoke. "I'd like to suggest, if you're willing, David, that you let me support you. I'm a licensed therapist with an emphasis on trauma recovery and family systems. We could meet once a week at my office. I won't charge you. How does that sound?"

David replied, "I'd like that."

"Will this work, Will?" the vet asked me.

"Yes. The courts usually want at least ten hours of community service. I think if we put in David's reparative plan that he's seeing a counselor for ten hours, the judge will allow that. I'll also talk to the university's judicial affairs officer overseeing David's case and advocate for this plan," I said.

"What about the essay?" asked David.

"How about if you and I work together on that? Tell your professor you want to do this. I suggest not telling her what it's for, just that you want to do it. I can at least proofread it for you," I said.

"I think that's it," I concluded. "But before we close our circle, I want to thank you for gathering and sharing your experience, perspectives, and support for David. David, is there anything you'd like to say before we disperse?"

David looked up. "I don't know what to say other than I don't feel so alone. You shared your own stories. I feel your support. We talked about healing. Your support of me started that healing."

I met with David three weeks after his conference to discuss his work with Jeff, the veteran. He said, "Jeff is helping me to understand why I get triggered when I feel threatened. We're working on some strategies."

I was filled with admiration for the progress David had made. But he was still at risk of being suspended from the university. I made a call to his discipline hearing officer to explain the work that we had done in our sessions, the reparative agreement, and the counseling that David was doing to work on the underlying issues for his behavior. I explained my view that he'd been through enough already and didn't need to be punished by the school. The hearing officer agreed, and his eventual appeal was successful. The court also dropped his charges.

To me, this case illustrates what happens when being bullied as a child goes unaddressed, and how a restorative dialogue can be a useful intervention. David was essentially acting out an unreconciled experience of being bullied when he "snapped" into violence. He was reenacting an old script based on false core beliefs—that if he didn't defend himself aggressively, he would be perceived as a coward—which were a direct result of being bullied. In our sessions, we were able to make the connection between David's violence and the violence that was done to him.

I've found that there are two fundamental principles that have to be in place when using restorative circles or dialogues to address bullying: *accountability* and *empathy*. In this context, "accountability" is not only about holding the wrongdoer accountable for their destructive impact, but also *"the ability to account for"* the under-lying reasons, issues, and conditions that compelled the bullying behavior—often mental health issues related to past trauma, fam-ily dynamics, and the culture and social norms that allow bullying to be okay. Empathy begins with taking the time to fully under-stand the "felt impact" of bullying on the physical, mental, and emotional health of the survivor(s), but also on a larger culture of the social environment—i.e., the community in which the bullying took place.

It's been my experience that when these two practices—empathy and accountability—are implemented, over time a larger culture of respect and transparency is fostered in the institution, and inci-dents of bullying decrease.

One of the gifts of a restorative justice conference in general is that it gives us the opportunity and the ability to discover the underlying issues, reasons, and circumstances that may have com-pelled a violation. The conversation can be a window into individual and social psychology. Doing that with a balance of accountability and healing is key. Yes, we accounted for the damage that David's reactions caused as a perpetrator of harm. But we also accounted for his suffering and pain.

In David's case, our circle helped to contest how David viewed himself as "the reason why" his beating happened, as well as con-testing the meta-social narrative that bullying is a normal part of growing up, and that violent retaliation is an acceptable response. Instead, our circle framed bullying as an act of violence and viola-tion, trauma that required healing. When others shared their own experience, David's story became our story.

2.

Transforming School Culture

Restorative justice is increasingly being taken up by K–12 principals and entire school districts as a "whole school" approach to building trust, empathy, and belonging within schools and thereby improving the overall school culture. As the story from Michael Beyer illustrates, by making schools a kinder and more connected place, restorative practices can be foundational for transforming the climate for learning—and with it, academic performance.

My Horrific 9/11 Good Day

Robert Spicer

I have worked as a consultant and trainer of restorative practices in school systems around the United States for twenty-five years. However, the most important lesson I learned about restorative justice came from a handful of third graders in my first year as a public-school teacher.

I grew up in New York City, but my first job was in Chicago, teaching at the Sojourner Truth Elementary School in a tough neighborhood called Cabrini Green. Crime and neglect made for hostile living conditions there, so much so that "Cabrini Green" had become synonymous with the failures of public housing in the United States.

It was 2001. I was fresh out of Morehouse College and a rookie male teacher within a mostly female faculty. My mentors instructed me to assert control of the classroom, and never to show any emotion in front of my students, because they would take it as a sign of weakness. This was the era when zero tolerance discipline was taking root, dictating that if children misbehaved in a disruptive way, the school could suspend, expel, or even arrest them. It was seen as a way to help remove the troublemakers so that we could raise the test scores. I didn't want to suspend or expel children. I thought that if we just worked with them, as their teachers, they would comply. There was so much that young people didn't know.

On the morning of September 11, 2001, I was running late to school and arrived right before classes started. I noticed that my colleagues were huddled around the little TV in our teachers' office. One of them said, "Hey, you're late, Robert, so punch in. You've got to get your kids to class. But you should know that something's happening in your city—a plane just hit one of the World Trade towers. You might want to call and check on your family."

I hurried to get my class of third-grade students out of the gym, lined them up, and brought them upstairs to classroom 302. I had been their teacher for less than a week, but I had been forewarned that this was a low-functioning class. One teacher even gave me the names of some students I'd have to make sure toed the line and didn't get away with anything.

I got the students seated and then ducked into the little closet off the room and closed the door, so that I could call my parents. But I kept getting busy signals. I did not realize it at the time, but the second plane had by then hit the World Trade Center, knocking out one of New York City's crucial cell phone towers. There was no phone service.

As every call rang busy, I began to get frantic, teared up, and began to cry. Remembering my colleagues' warning, I knew I couldn't face my children in an emotional state, so I stayed in the closet, trying to collect myself.

At the time, we were using a curriculum that called for the students to sit together in a meeting area in the classroom to drill math skills and science skills. I would lead the drills and the children would answer. When I failed to materialize from the closet to start the day's instruction, a boy named Antoine took it upon himself to lead the drill.

Antoine was one of the students my colleague had told me I should watch closely. Through a crack in the door of the closet, I watched as he rummaged through my desk and found my pointer. He went through the math skills with his classmates. Then he asked, "What's today's date?"

Someone said, "September 11, 2001."

"Write it on the blackboard." One of the students went up and wrote it in his best penmanship.

"Okay, what planet are we on? See, we are on Jupiter," Antoine said, to laughter from the rest of the class. Then he said, "No, really, what planet are we on?"

"Earth!"

"Go point to it."

And then, "What's the temperature?" Another boy went to the window, opened it up, and put his hand out and said, "It's warm."

"No, no, no, give me a number."

"I say 75."

"Okay, move the thermometer," Antoine said, gesturing to the toy thermometer on the wall of the classroom we were using to learn about temperatures.

Antoine then moved on to their times tables, mimicking me as they went through the ones and then the twos. As I listened from the closet, I was thinking, "I just met this kid. How does he know this so well?"

Antoine then moved the children to the reading rug, where each morning a student would pick their favorite book, and I would read it to the class. The only book that Antoine could read, his favorite, was *No, David*, by David Shannon. It's about a boy who gets into a lot of trouble, with his mother continually having to say, "No, David," throughout the whole book. Antoine was sitting in my rocking chair, fully occupying the role of teacher. There he was, perched in my rocking chair as he looked down and asked one of the children, "What's your favorite page?"

There's a part of this book that all the kids loved. He turned to the page where David is outside, running naked. "Do you know why I chose that page?" he asked. "Because when I was a kid, I ran outside naked, and my mama gave me a whooping." The kids all burst into laughter, and I started laughing a little bit, even through my tears.

I sat there in the closet and thought, *Wait a minute. Is this the class that people were telling me was filled with low-functioning troublemakers?* At this point, I had opened the closet door halfway. I could hear and see the students, and they could see me, too. They had inferred that something was terribly wrong with their teacher and were clearly giving me time to compose myself.

Eventually Antoine came over to the closet and grabbed my hand. He looked up at me and said, "Mr. Spicer, could you come over to the reading rug? You want to talk?" And so I did. By that time, tears were running down my face, and I was just a mess. I sat down in my rocking chair.

Antoine sat down next to me, and then the children asked, "Who did it to you, Mr. Spicer? Whoever did it, we're going to beat him up right now."

I said, "Nobody did anything to me. Something terrible has happened in New York, and I can't get in touch with my mom and my dad. Some planes have hit two buildings there, and I'm not able to communicate with my family. I'm scared."

They all kind of looked around at each other. And then a boy named Percy got up, raised his hand, and said, "Mr. Spicer, I've been talking to the other students, and we have a question."

I said, "What's that?"

He said, "We didn't know you had a mom and dad."

I said, "Yeah, I do." I showed them a picture of my mom and dad.

A few of them looked and said, "Oh, you look like your mom," or "You look like your dad." And then we just started talking about our parents.

Some of their parents had passed away. Some of their parents were in jail, and their grandparents were raising them. We all talked about how much we cared for and loved our parents. The conversation was very much like the way we start peacemaking circles in restorative justice, except that there was no talking piece. Children just went around the circle and each spoke in turn.

Then Percy got up again and said, "Mr. Spicer?"

And I said, "Yes."

He said, "Well, I see the Sears Tower out our window. Are they going to hit that building, too?"

I said, "No, no. I think this is something that's only happening in New York, but if anything happens, I'm not leaving you. I'm here with you, and I'll protect you."

A couple of them said, "Good, because I would hate to have to fight whoever it is that crashed into the building." That caused a big laugh.

And then, finally, we got to the moment when we had to get back to our desks. Percy stood up again and said, "Whenever I feel bad or I feel sad, I get a hug from my grandma, and I feel better. Can we hug you? Maybe if we hug you, that'll make you feel better."

Now, there is a very important rule in schools that the kids are not supposed to touch you, and you are not supposed to touch them, even for a hug. But I needed a hug. And so, I got in the middle of the reading rug while all thirty of those children surrounded and hugged me. And then I felt a pinch on my backside! I turned around and I looked down to see Percy.

"Percy, what you doing?"

He said, "I just wanted to make sure it was real."

"What? My butt?"

He said, "Yeah," and with that, all the children just fell down in hysterical laughter. I fell down laughing, too.

Percy was trying to make sure I was a real human being, just like him. That interaction set the stage for so many great things that we were able to do in class that year, and a lot of those young people went on to great things themselves. Sadly, Percy passed away from an asthma attack when he was in middle school. I try to honor him by bringing his spirit into everything I do, because he was such a sweet young man.

But it was also at that moment that I realized that what the adults were teaching me about discipline was wrong. The tools the school was giving me were not about getting to know these children on a basic human level. They were all about control, power, and "Do what I say" as a form of directive instruction. I learned that day that there's a better way, and that is to build a *foundational relationship* with all the students, in a stance of mutual respect. This is a fundamental tenet of restorative justice.

I would use those concepts and my teaching skills in a later position I took with the Community Justice for Youth Institute in Chicago, where I directed a program called Community Panels for Youth. Through their efforts we helped hundreds of youth by restoring them to right relationship with the communities they harmed. The community volunteers would listen to their cases and support young people on their journey toward healing, accountability, and reconciliation. Once the youth finished their process with the Community Panels, the court would drop the charges.

I was later introduced to peacemaking circles by Kay Pranis, a godmother of restorative justice, and became a trained peace circle keeper and practitioner. I would later take these skills back into the Chicago Public Schools, where I was hired to support the turn-around efforts at one of their high schools. I immediately transformed my office into the "Peace Room" and offered peace circles and other strategies to support the school leadership's overall plan for violence reduction, proactive responses to conflict, and a school community based on the philosophy of restorative justice.

I now work with schools nationally to support their adoption of social-emotional learning and restorative justice programming. I get to give back to the very age group that taught me so much in my role as a schoolteacher twenty-five years ago. I wouldn't have been ready to undertake what would be my life's work if I hadn't had that profound experience with Antoine, Percy, and that beautiful group of children in room 302 at Sojourner Truth Elementary School. They showed a young educator compassion on one of the hardest days of his life. When I think back, it was on that horrific day, September 11, 2001, that I learned the power of gathering in a circle to share our emotions, reveal our humanity, and develop a relationship of honesty and trust on which other good things can be built.

Building Bridges over Troubled Water

Cheryl Newkirk

I am a social worker by trade and have worked in the private sector as a clinical therapist, in the public sector as a school-based mental health clinician, and for over fifteen years as a school social worker in every level of public education you can imagine. To say that I adore our youth is to put it lightly. They reenergize me in a way that keeps me alive and healthy. Their joy is contagious, and even in their less than appealing moments, I would be hard-pressed to choose an adult over a young person.

However, after almost two decades working with young people, in both their greatest and most challenging moments, it became evident to me that I was fighting a losing battle of rescue. I had been pulling children out of a dangerous river over and over again, providing them with life vests, floats, flippers, ropes, whatever it took to keep them out of the water or at least afloat. But I was finding myself pulling the same children out of the river again and again. I couldn't figure out why. I was working so hard.

It was a bittersweet decision to shift gears five years ago from working with children to supporting the adults in my school district. As the project facilitator for school climate transformation in the Syracuse City School District, I have been focusing on building the skills of adult staff to implement restorative practices with the goal of establishing healthier environments within our schools. What became immediately evident to me in this position was that these children were not metaphorically "falling into the river." They were being pushed in. Sometimes inadvertently, and other times with intention. Either way, I finally came to the conclusion that the children were not the problem. It was us. The adults. We had some growing to do.

One day, I was approached with an opportunity to provide a onetime workshop demonstrating what a morning circle could look like for a small group of staff members in an elementary school.

"We've heard Cheryl can do it, and we'd like her to come show us she can do it here." I initially thought this was a flattering invitation. As it turns out, the communication was really intended to say, "Prove it. Prove restorative circles can work with *these* kids." Our children were experiencing anxiety, emotional outbursts, and having difficulty building trust in others, all as a result of past traumatic experiences reflective of their struggle to feel safe and secure. However, these pain-based behaviors were not being viewed through a trauma-informed lens. Rather, students were being disciplined for behaviors, most of which were neurologically out of their control, and punitive consequences were presumably the solution.

While circles had been established in some of the classroom settings, the experience was less community building and more lecture-based. Perhaps the adults were afraid in some ways— afraid of what they could not control, either the behaviors or the children themselves.

Syracuse has thirty-four public schools, each with a unique culture that influences how restorative practices are received and implemented by their staff and students. The system provides a microcosm of what we see nationwide, in that a simple misunderstanding of restorative practice can affect each tier of implementation. Many people hear "restorative practices" and think it's purely about recovering from an incident that caused harm. However, restorative practices really begin at the universal level, with community building, relationship development, and human understanding.

One school community in our district was desperate for change and ready for a solution that would support both their students and staff. This was a dual-language elementary school struggling with low academic scores, low attendance, and high numbers of disciplinary incidents. The administrative team, along with the Student Support Team, had identified several fifth-grade students in need of individualized intervention. At the start of our discussion, the focus was on these students, but soon we realized that the challenges extended beyond these few; the school had a community-wide issue.

The school had experimented with restorative circles in the past; however, consistent with a common misunderstanding of restorative practices, these circles had been limited to reactively responding to disciplinary incidents or other conflicts rather than proactive efforts to foster unity and community. I suggested implementing community-building circles as a way of *preventing* conflicts in the first instance by strengthening relationships. The idea resonated with the team, and soon we set out to integrate forty-five-minute circle sessions into each fifth-grade classroom every week.

Since time is a limited resource in every school, the schedule was complicated at first. With some convincing, the administrative team agreed to allow some grace with academic instruction and permitted a rotating schedule between different subject areas, reducing how much content any one class was actually missing. This seemed like a logical compromise, given that teachers were already losing instructional time in responding to conflicts between students, redirecting behaviors during and after transitions, and providing multiple reminders during class.

Our community-building circles had a simple, straightforward structure. They began with a review of the Circle Agreements, a Mindful Moment (to help ground circle participants in the space), an Opening (usually a quote or poem read by a student focused on the topic of the day), a Check In (to allow everyone to share how they are feeling at the start of circle), an Activity, a Check Out, and a Closing (a riddle that classrooms were directed to solve together as a "team," encouraging team building and community engagement outside of the circle space).

Circle Agreements were the same for each circle and reviewed by circle participants each week: Respect the Talking Piece (one speaker at a time, and it is okay to pass); Listen to Understand, not Respond; Stories Stay, Lessons Leave; and Speak from the Heart. Review of these agreements was intentional, and time was spent to allow student participants to describe what the agreements meant to them and to ensure clear understanding of the group norms.

The transition wasn't seamless. Initially, both students and teachers were hesitant. Students had previously experienced circles as punitive measures, while teachers had limited exposure to them. As noted, conflict resolution circles had been attempted in response to problems among students or within the classroom structure. However, without implementation of proactive community-building circles in advance of these responsive circles, the effectiveness of conflict resolution circles can be minimal.

Many students passed the talking piece on their turn, choosing not to share. While this was in line with our Circle Agreements, it certainly communicated that they did not feel brave enough in the space to open up and speak . . . yet. Teachers communicated something similar with their body language and, at times, outright avoidance; some found other things to do during the scheduled circle, and others opted to manage behaviors in the hallways that were unrelated to their classroom community. Staff and students were bringing in their own biases and preconceived ideas about circles based on past experiences. It was up to us as a community to build something different and better, where everyone could feel empowered together. With gentle coaching and a positive approach, attitudes began to shift.

In the first few weeks, instead of diving into deep topics, we focused on community-building games. *Big Wind Blows* allowed students to engage in kinesthetic movement while simultaneously sharing information about themselves in a low-risk setting, building skills such as listening, public speaking, and healthy competition. Students were given opportunities to ask questions of one another to discover commonalities among themselves. While their questions initially focused on physical appearance ("Big Wind Blows for everyone wearing black pants"), they evolved into questions focused on other aspects of identity (for example, "Big Wind Blows for everyone who has more than three siblings"). *Dance Telephone*, another movement-based game, highlighted skills such as patience, perseverance, and communication as students attempted to communicate dance moves from one person to the next, leaving much to interpretation. Another game, *1-2-3-Hooray*, challenged students in pairs and supported skills such as focus and kindness, while also allowing them to practice use of a growth mind-set and celebration of mistakes. Every game played was intentional, although if you asked the students, they would have explained they were just having a great time together. They laughed together and grew to appreciate being with one another in a new way.

Each of these activities encouraged movement and humor. Gradually, students became more comfortable sharing personal experiences and discussing topics like perspective and friendship. This newfound understanding led to improved behavioral dynamics among peers. In another activity, we focused on perspective using an object in the center of the circle, asking students to identify what they saw, and then hearing the different responses and the significant variances offered by participants. When students were asked, "So who is lying about what they see?" and no one was lying, then asked, "So who is wrong about what they say they see?" and no one was wrong, it opened up a new dialogue about perspective, and how two people can experience the same moment in very different ways, and report very different observations about it, yet neither of them is incorrect.

Eventually, we began exploring topics such as empathy and equity, and how these ideas were related to the district's Code of Conduct. The discussion about empathy directly connects to the discussion about perspective: When you are able to see something from someone else's point of view it often helps you to feel how they might feel or understand their circumstances differently. With empathy comes the ability to be more equitable, in which case we discussed that fair is indeed not equal, but rather fair means everyone gets what they need.

The beauty of these discussions is that they are predominantly student-led. While the questions are posed by the adult circle keeper—adhering to the circle norm of the talking piece, which is passed around and all participants have an opportunity to share without being interrupted—the students share insightful ideas about each topic with little prompting. They set the standards high for themselves, engaging in higher-level critical thinking on their own.

As the circles progressed, students began to take ownership of the process itself. Each week when I arrived, they meticulously set up the circle center with care, established the agreements, and ensured everyone had a chance to speak using a talking piece. Even during games, they prioritized safety and fairness, enforcing rules to maintain a supportive community.

Of course, there were challenges along the way. In the context of a dual-language school, some activities required modification for students who were not fluent in English. However, we quickly adapted, ensuring all students could participate fully in subsequent sessions. What was notable is that, even when it was difficult for some students to engage due to lack of modification, the students did not respond with disruptive behavior, which one might expect. They articulated a need for help from trusted adults and peers, demonstrating important social-emotional skills even in those frustrating moments.

Still, some students struggled to grant that trust. One fifth grader refused to join our classroom circle for the first three months. For many weeks, he would stand in the doorway looking out into the hallway, almost as if he was standing guard. After some time he started sitting at a desk in proximity to the circle with a laptop and earbuds. And then one day, seemingly without rhyme or reason, he sat in our circle. He passed the talking piece, joined the game, and checked in and out with the group. He just needed time to trust the process. I appreciated his patience, and I believe he appreciated our perseverance and consistency as a supportive community.

In another classroom, by contrast, a young man expressed immediate enthusiasm for the circle process. Each time I entered the room, nothing else in the world mattered to him but to establish the circle space and get started with the dialogue. He was more than happy to open up about his entire personal life to the circle community beginning on day one. He offered the perfect example of a student who was desperate for a space to talk and share and build relationship.

In fact, we found that many students, even those who were more shy than this young man, were in desperate need of adult help and attention but had not felt safe enough at school to share what they needed. In so many instances, we heard about the hardships our students carry with them on a day-to-day basis. One student shared that she was having a particularly bad week and did not want to share why, but that she was happy to be in circle because that's where she felt happy to be with her friends. Other student participants asked if she was okay and if there was anything they could do to help but never pressured her to share her story. However, by the end of the circle, she felt comfortable enough to share that it was the anniversary week of her brother's death, and her entire family hurts, which makes it hard to be at home. For a student who did not often openly share her feelings or show emotion, sharing this story through tears in her eyes was a huge step forward in trusting her peers.

Another time, during a circle discussion about empathy, a student who had been targeted by bullies in the past mentioned that he would show empathy and support for anyone who had been bullied by classmates—"anyone who is called fat, ugly, or stupid." As adults, we knew he was reflecting on his own experiences. His peers demonstrated immediate empathy: One student shared that he, too, had experienced bullying when he first moved here because he did not speak English, and it was very hard for him. Sharing these moments of vulnerability with one another took courage from the students and an understanding that the students had built a brave space together.

Many students shared that circle was the best part of their week. When the school schedule was "too full" for circle due to testing or field trips, several expressed how they missed the time to connect with each other and to share things about their families: who is the first one up in their house, who the last one to go to bed, who has to share a room, who has had to grieve a loved one, and so much more.

The overall impact of these circles was profound. Academic performance among the fifth graders improved significantly, and disciplinary incidents declined even as they trended upward in other grade levels. Fifth-grade attendance for the 2023–2024 school year averaged 4 percent higher than the school-wide average after the adoption of community circles in December. The positive shift was also reflected in the school climate surveys, where students and staff reported feeling more connected and supported. The measure of feeling safe at school among fifth graders increased 7 percent from the previous school year, and 63 percent of students reported a decrease in online and in-school bullying and said that they were able to find support and help from an adult in school. Relationships among students and teachers improved as well, with 81 percent indicating they would be excited to have their teacher again, and 82 percent stating they felt respected by their teacher. Seventy-two percent said that their teacher recognized their social-emotional needs. Each of these scores was an improvement over the previous year's school climate survey.

Word of the circles' success spread to other grade levels, prompting invitations from the fourth- and first-grade teacher teams. Community Circles took place in one fourth-grade classroom for the final three months of school, after the teacher said that "her students needed it; they are just not nice to each other." By the end of the final circle, the same teacher reported that every single week that we held circle, she cried because she was learning something new about her students that helped her to see them in a new light. She learned about how hard they were working every day. She learned how much they enjoyed being in school despite the pain-based behaviors they demonstrated in her classroom. She learned they slept on couches, which was a step up from the floor they had been sleeping on the last several months, and how much more rested they felt coming in each morning. The same teacher also noticed the students demonstrating acts of kindness to one another that she never thought possible. Students who were once unable to sit near one another due to threats of safety and concerns of physical aggression were now greeting one another in the morning and offering helpful reminders to keep the other on track. Other students were laughing at one another's jokes, offering high fives and congratulations when someone got the answer right, and listening while others shared—all behaviors in line with the Circle Agreements. The students had embraced the values from the circle community and translated them into their classroom.

One first-grade classroom was able to schedule circles for the final month of school, and the shift in mind-set was almost immediate. The teacher was similar to many in that she was asking for conflict resolution and "lecture-based" circles, rather than community building. However, she quickly realized that when the students used movement-based and community-building games to improve their sense of self in the classroom, their behavior improved and the need for responsive circles dissipated. She reported that she was excited to bring the tools she had learned into the following school year. While implementation wasn't as thorough in grades one and four due to their start late in the school year, the interest sparked training opportunities for future integration.

The change in outlook and behavior wasn't limited to the students—it extended to the staff. Circles were so successful that the administration asked me to organize a full-staff training session on community building. It was initially met with skepticism and anxiety by some participants; however, by the end of the session, these skeptics were expressing their newfound enthusiasm for community-building activities. Staff were laughing together, dancing, smiling, and, most important, building community.

As educators, we are in the business of teaching academic subjects to children. Students enter our doors not knowing and are expected to leave "knowing." But knowing what? The expectations of schools have shifted in many ways over the last several decades, and teachers must adapt to diverse learning styles, incorporate technology into the classroom, and support students' emotional and social needs. There's also a greater emphasis on inclusivity and personalized learning, as well as accountability through standardized testing and data-driven instruction. Teachers are now expected to be mentors and facilitators of holistic student development.

We are often discussing new ways to instruct curriculum but not considering the importance of our universal practices to establish a healthy school climate in which that learning can take place. When we use community circles, we help students develop skills such as self-awareness, self-management, social awareness, relationship building, and responsible decision making. These skills are essential for students to navigate social interactions, manage emotions effectively, and make responsible choices both in and out of school.

Community building also fosters a sense of belonging and inclusivity within the school environment. When students feel connected to their peers, teachers, and the school community as a whole, they are more likely to engage actively in learning and feel motivated to succeed. A positive school climate also reduces instances of bullying and negative behaviors.

Research indicates a strong correlation between social-emotional learning and improved academic performance. When students have well-developed social and emotional skills, they are better able to focus on learning, manage stress, and persist through challenges. Additionally, a supportive school community encourages academic risk taking and collaboration among students.

By promoting circles and fostering a strong sense of community, schools can also proactively address behavioral issues. When students feel valued and supported, they are less likely to engage in disruptive behaviors or act out. Community-building circles strengthen the relationships between teachers and students. When teachers understand their students' social and emotional needs, they can create a more supportive and nurturing learning environment. This, in turn, enhances trust and communication within the classroom.

What began as targeted support for a few fifth-grade students evolved into a school-wide initiative that transformed relationships and nurtured a more inclusive school culture. Through proactive community-building circles, we both addressed individual needs and fostered a supportive environment where every voice was valued and heard. We discovered why children were falling into the water. And as a community, we built a bridge.

What Restorative Justice Teaches the Next Generation

Mark Carey

I am a former president of the American Probation and Parole Association, but the story I want to tell is not about criminal justice, but about restorative justice in a school setting. It is not really my story; I heard it from a teacher who had been in one of our early trainings. She asked if I would share her story. Every now and then when I am feeling frustrated because things aren't changing fast enough for me, I'll read this story again.

I work in an elementary school. I've been involved in education for twenty years, and I love the kids. They are so full of energy and optimism. They truly represent hope. Besides that, they will pay for my nursing home one day, so I'd better feel this way about them. I like to tell the kids that each gray hair represents a child I helped grow into a mature teenager or young adult, and I look forward to a complete head of gray hair someday. At that point, I will retire. As long as I have any brunette strands left, I intend on working.

I attended a restorative justice conference about four years ago. I was instantly attracted to the values and principles, and it didn't take me long to think it might be useful in a school setting. I had no idea how useful it would end up being.

We trained as many staff and teachers as were interested. For some, it took hold; for others, it was just another training. We started with a core group of trained educators who met on a regular basis to brainstorm how we could apply this to a school setting. It didn't take us long to realize that it would probably be most useful around student conflict issues. Too many kids were getting hurt emotionally or physically over spats and bullying. We'd discipline the aggressors only to have to deal with more of the same later on. So, we put into place a circle process to address inter-student conflict. Our hope was that it might provide an avenue for healing relationships and reduce the amount of future conflict. While it did not work perfectly all the time, it worked better than I had ever imagined.

Conflict after conflict was addressed in a circle process, where the students handled their own affairs with only minor guidance from us. The key to using circles is that the students agree on how they think they should act with each other while in circle. In our circles they named their values and quickly decided how they would use them for each circle, which were not altogether different from what we adults generally come up with; they just expressed them differently, more like six- or seven-year-olds. They used phrases like "be nice" or "have fun" instead of what we might say, but it was really the same. We were having good success with restoring relationships and reducing tensions. But then something happened that reminded me that all of this work pays big dividends. In fact, it was a defining moment for me.

I was monitoring the playground during the break immediately after lunch, which I do every Tuesday and Thursday. I was chatting with a colleague of mine and wasn't paying close attention to what was going on near the swing set. All of a sudden, Lisa came running up to me. Lisa is a sweet, precocious six-year-old girl. Her family life is not the greatest. When I first met her, I took a liking to her immediately. We developed this kind of competitive relationship where we try to outdo each other with kindness: I'll tell her how smart she is, and she'll tell me that I should be the president of the United States; or I'll tell her how lovely she looks, and she'll reply that I remind her of a princess. Anyway, on this afternoon, she ran up to me and said, "Ms. McCarthy, Ms. McCarthy, quick . . . I need the talking piece." She was bouncing up and down on her toes and back to the balls of her feet, anxious to get this talking piece and run back to her friends. Not quite knowing what this was all about, I pulled out of my pocket the talking piece—a fluorescent dinosaur—and handed it to her. She sprinted out of earshot before I could recover. Then, around the corner of the building, I witnessed something incredible. I saw Lisa run up to a group of five other kids her age and instructed them to sit down in a circle. She then began to facilitate a circle process.

I watched this with incredulity. And then it hit me: Yes, we were implementing a program through which conflicts were reduced, and relationships were restored; yes, we were addressing harm when it occurred, but we were also actually teaching the *next* generation how to resolve conflict before it gets out of hand. We were doing the best form of prevention by using an experiential approach to teach our kids a set of values that upholds dignity and respect and imparts skills that they can use in all settings. Think about it! It is the gift that keeps on giving to each generation that follows. We now have six- and seven-year-old children using a process for conflict resolution and respectful communication that adults with decades of experience still don't know how to do. When I stood there watching those kids sitting in a circle right there on the playground, I thought to myself, *I love this work. This is worth every single gray hair.* I might just have to rethink my retirement date.

Transforming Whole School Culture

Michael Beyer

The first time I visited Morrill School, I was a senior manager in the Performance Management Department in the central office of the Chicago Public Schools. I was assigned a portfolio of schools that had been deemed "failing"; Morrill was one of many. The school had been on academic probation for over a decade, and rumors were swirling that the district was going to close it.

Every week I met with a select group of teachers at a folding table in Morrill's auditorium. I developed a rapport with several teachers, and when the long-serving principal announced she was retiring, they helped convince members of the Local School Council to award me the principal contract.

The summer before I officially became the principal, we invited our neighbors, George and Nancy Michaels, over for dinner in our backyard. When I mentioned the challenges at Morrill, Nancy told me about her work implementing restorative justice, a concept I had heard of in passing but wasn't very familiar with. Her brief explanation of restorative justice matched my personal philosophy of working with students. She offered to help me, and we scheduled a meeting at the school.

When I decided to leave the classroom and become a school administrator, I was confident the primary cause of underperforming schools was the leadership of the principal. But in the course of my training as a principal and my doctoral studies, I also came to understand the important and interdependent role of teacher practices, school climate and culture, instructional leadership, and community partnerships. In other words, it was rarely one aspect of a school that caused it to falter.

I knew Morrill had issues related to student discipline before I became the principal. I witnessed it every time I visited the school. Lining students up in the hallway between classes was common in many schools, but at Morrill, the teachers would also direct the students to stand "in their square" on the checkered linoleum floors, one square away from their peers. Teachers explained this was to keep students from violating their peers' personal body space and prevent physical altercations.

It wasn't just this practice that seemed odd to me. Every teacher, even the quietest and nicest ones, yelled at students. Yelling and shouting at students, even those in primary grades, was the norm. Students were required to wear uniforms, which consisted of navy blue pants and shirts. When students came to school out of uniform, teachers sent them to the office, where they were given a bright orange prison jumpsuit that had "loaner" written in large letters on the back. The assistant principal I inherited bragged about how she collected students who had earned after-school detention and lined them up against the wall in the cafeteria at the end of the day, for the entire student body to see. Public shaming and embarrassment were the *modus operandi* of the school's leadership, and the school-to-prison pipeline was more visible and palpable in operation here than in any school I had ever experienced.

When I began to analyze the school's data, a clear pattern emerged: Out of the thirty teachers, a handful accounted for over half of the student discipline referrals. Some teachers believed that when a student disrespected their authority, the student should be referred to the principal's office. Other teachers believed it was their responsibility to develop a positive and supportive classroom culture in which students learned to respect the teacher and one another. In these classrooms, the teacher remained the authority, but students learned to resolve issues together, like a family. It was a difference in perspectives that led to vastly different outcomes.

The facilities and grounds of the school were dismal. The hallways were dim like caves. Most classrooms had cracked paint with mismatched chairs and desks that looked like they had been acquired at a rummage sale. Teachers wrote on old chalkboards and used overhead projectors with transparencies. Bathroom doors remained propped open so teachers could monitor student behavior. Soap and paper towels were rarely available. Many of the bathroom stalls were missing doors, and the stall doors that existed were too short to give students privacy.

Once the school day ended, the parking lot emptied. Only a handful of assistants lived in the community. Faculty and staff avoided being at the school after hours or on the weekends; they never visited student homes, walked the community, or frequented the local businesses and restaurants. I realized this in the first month as principal, when I arrived early at the school on a beautiful fall day. Students had not yet arrived, so I decided to walk to the local Dunkin Donuts, three blocks away. A teaching assistant who lived in the community looked at me and exasperatingly stated, "You can't walk there, Principal Beyer, it's dangerous!" Admittedly, being a white man, six feet tall and having spent time in the military, I wasn't fazed by much. Yet the idea that walking a few blocks at seven in the morning was dangerous seemed ridiculous. After that day I made a habit of walking to the Dunkin Donuts every morning. On my daily walks I saw students accompanying siblings to school, observed their parents heading to work, and got to know the hustle and bustle of the community.

Turning Morrill School around was a tall order. I recognized at least four areas that required focus: student discipline, teaching and learning, facilities, and community relations. Were it not for the partnership with Nancy Michaels and Roosevelt University's Mansfield Institute for Social Justice and Transformation, I would have tackled school discipline with one hand tied behind my back. But thanks to Nancy and her colleagues, during my first summer we scheduled a large peace circle in the library. We invited parents, teachers, staff, and middle school students. Participants were hesitant to speak at first, but eventually several shared their experiences and desires for their students and community. That was a first, small step.

We made restorative justice training a cornerstone for the next several years. Every teacher received training, which I also attended with my assistant principal. We paid the Mansfield Institute to hire college students as restorative justice facilitators to staff a peace room to resolve discipline problems during the school day, which was a welcome relief from having students lined up outside my office all day. The facilitators helped address situations between students as well as between students and teachers. I worked closely with the college students, learning what they saw and heard in classrooms and hallways, which usually supported my hunches about which teachers were ready and willing to adopt a new perspective and practice, and which were not.

By midyear I began to have conversations with teachers who did not show progress in adopting restorative justice methods. Many of them seemed incapable of change, but it was usually because of their beliefs. The teachers tended to use coded language about "those" students and their "inability" to behave and their "disinterest" in learning. I invited those teachers to one-on-one conversations in my office, with the door closed, and let them know the school culture was changing, and that they would need to embrace the change or seek positions elsewhere.

By the end of the first year, the low-performing, high-discipline teachers had moved on. This accounted for about 54 percent of the faculty. As the teachers left, I searched high and low for Black and Hispanic candidates as I wanted our students to have people with whom they could identify. One of the teachers I hired during my first year was Rashad Talley. Black male teachers are rare in education these days, especially in elementary and middle schools. When I left Morrill, he became the first Black principal of the school.

Rashad joined the school during my first year and witnessed the school in transition. He described the change this way:

> Before implementing restorative justice, Morrill was characterized by a sterile and punitive atmosphere. Discipline was primarily focused on punishment rather than understanding and addressing root causes of behavior. The environment often felt rigid and authoritarian, lacking empathy and opportunities for students to learn from their mistakes in a constructive manner.
>
> After implementing restorative justice, Morrill transformed into a community where family support and collaboration became priorities for student success. The culture shifted toward empathy and understanding, focusing on repairing harm and building relationships rather than punitive measures. Students felt supported and empowered to take responsibility for their actions in a nurturing environment aimed at their holistic development.

Another teacher, Octavia Sansing, concurred. She joined in my second year, and our restorative justice methods were still being ironed out. According to Octavia, before restorative justice was fully adopted, students operated from a place of denial. When accused of misbehavior, they would respond with "I didn't do it!" or "Why are you picking on me?" After everyone was trained and our peace room was fully operational, the tone of the school changed. Teachers and students would work together to "get to the core of the root cause," as Octavia remembers. Restorative justice not only taught students to be personally accountable to themselves and others, but it also gave them voice to express themselves. This aspect of restorative justice is not recognized or appreciated as much as it could be.

In order to accept personal accountability, the voice, experience, and perspective of the victim must be heard. In turn, the voice, experience, and perspective of the offender needs to be shared and understood. This does not mean we accept their actions as justified. Rather, by enabling offenders to be able to identify and speak about the "why" that led to their actions, we enable them to realize and learn from their mistakes. If offenders are backed into a corner and threatened with punishment, denial is the natural stance. If, instead, offenders can demonstrate they are learning and changing and have the opportunity to make amends to the victim, authentic accountability can be achieved.

When I first began as principal only a handful of parents and grandparents participated in the Parent Mentor organization, where the idea was to have parents and grandparents in the school to assist teachers and monitor students during lunch and recess. Estella Bautista was a mother whose four children graduated from Morrill. She was also the Parent Mentor coordinator for fifteen years. Working with Mrs. Bautista, we grew our Parent Mentor program to include over twenty parents and grandparents, with a better, more equitable representation of Latino and Black families. We also sent Mrs. Bautista and all the parent mentors to restorative justice training.

Mrs. Bautista described the school before restorative justice as "Chaos all the time. Whatever the previous administration was doing wasn't working. Students were always suspended, but they wouldn't be at home, they'd be in the streets. After restorative justice, suspensions were rare, and they were in school, so students knew the adults were watching them. Restorative justice helped change the whole community. We were happy."

Similarly, the philosophy of restorative justice transformed relationships in the school. The coordinator of Teen REACH, David Castro, took the foundation of restorative justice to new heights. By my fourth year as principal, David Castro had empowered the middle school students to lead trainings with teachers, sharing student perspectives on how classes could instill more equity, respect, student voice, and accountability. David also worked closely with the school administration, ensuring we knew when he disagreed with our decisions and actions, serving as a counterweight set of checks and balances to our official authority. His program empowered some of the best students in the school to become community leaders, but he also helped work with some of the most challenging students, many of whom would have been lost to the streets without his program.

After four years of relentless effort from everyone, our school had been transformed from inside to out, and the results showed. Enrollment, attendance, and test scores were the highest they had been in years, and student behavioral infractions were at an all-time low. Faculty and staff regularly met at a local restaurant on 63rd Street, Garifuna Flava, for happy hours after school. For the first time in a generation, our school achieved the highest rating possible for the district, taking it off academic probation and removing the threat of closure.

Here are the lessons I learned from implementing restorative justice at Morrill:

1. **Change takes time and resources.** We were one of the first schools to implement restorative justice. When Chicago Public Schools later altered the student code of conduct and disciplinary process to embrace restorative justice processes, they provided minimal training and almost no resources for implementation. In contrast at Morrill, we invested by sending every teacher, staff, administrator, and parent volunteer to restorative justice training. We paid stipends to the college students working as facilitators, hired and trained a full-time restorative justice coordinator, and worked closely with community groups including Teen REACH and SWOP. It still took several years of learning, trying and failing, and adjusting to this new way of working before we felt we were getting it right.

2. **Changing mind-sets and behaviors is key.** Implementing new processes or policies might eventually lead to new mind-sets and behaviors, but too often this order of activities is like leading the proverbial horse to water and expecting it to drink. Training paired with authentic, courageous conversations needs to happen first. Some people don't want to be on your bus, and you need to let them off. Find and keep the people ready and willing to change their mind-sets and behaviors.

3. **Everyone's voice matters.** Empowering faculty, staff, students, and families to give feedback on processes and policies is uncomfortable for any leader, but it is essential. If people don't feel comfortable sharing their voices, you

haven't established a culture of trust. Empowering voices was key to my leadership. I was willing to be the least-smart person in the room if that meant people felt comfortable speaking out. And I trusted that by eliciting and incorporating honest feedback, I would make better decisions.

4. **Foster adaptive systems focused on adult learning.** In all our efforts, from improving facilities, designing and maintaining the green schoolyard, creating new instructional practices, and implementing restorative justice, we created feedback loops of communication that fostered adult learning. We admitted our mistakes and missteps and tried to do better. Never once did we believe a program was perfect out of the box. It probably helped that nothing we implemented was a "canned" product, and we had to co-create it. Everything needs to be adapted to local context and situations.

5. **School transformation is a multipronged effort.** Restorative justice was the first program we implemented but by no means the only or the last. We restored the facilities inside and out and the relationships with the community, and transformed the instructional practices and the curriculum. Too often schools focus on a single item to "fix," but it quickly becomes a game of whack-a-mole because of the dozens of other issues that pop up, distracting from their singular focus.

6. **Everyone deserves restorative justice.** I coached out half the staff, and terminated the employment of plenty of teachers, at least one being led out of the school by the police.[11] I also excluded some parents from entering the school due to their behavior. However, those were the last resorts, and we always tried to use restorative methods to build mutual trust, respect, and understanding that would lead to a col-

laborative effort to improve the situation and address root causes. It is unfortunate and ironic that schools are implementing restorative justice with students but holding employees accountable through authoritative processes.

Switching from a punitive form of discipline to restorative justice implicates not just a set of rules, but a set of beliefs. If you're a principal, and you believe children learn by being punished, then you're not going to believe in restorative justice. And it doesn't matter what the training or the policy from the district looks like, you're probably not going to do it very well, because in the back of your mind you're going to want to punish this child. And if the principal does not believe in restorative justice, then it's not going to be done well or it's going to take much longer.

We transformed the school through sweat, tears, and a variety of different initiatives. But had we not also embraced the mind-set and modeled the behaviors of restorative justice, I don't believe the other programs would have helped.

Part Two

Youthful Offending

3.

Understanding the Consequences of Offenses

As any parent knows, adolescents are self-focused beings, and as such often not cognizant of the impact of their actions on others. Restorative justice dialogues provide an opportunity for young people to hear directly from those who have been harmed. Understanding the consequences of one's behavior is the first step toward empathy and learning from one's mistakes. By offering young people support in holding themselves accountable to others and a chance to repair harm they have caused, restorative justice dialogues elicit more honesty from young people than does pure punishment, and supports greater creativity in correcting their behavior. By emphasizing adults' faith in—as well as high expectations of—young people, restorative justice emphasizes accountability to an entire community of people demonstrably invested in their success.

What I Learned About Youth Rehabilitation After Eighteen Years as a Cop

David Hines

I've been a cop for twenty-seven years in the greater Minneapolis area. I've worked as a patrol officer, an investigator, a crime prevention specialist, and held a lot of other jobs in the department. I've worked with many young people over the years, and before I retired, I served as the coordinator of a community restorative justice program housed within our police department.

Although I've become a strong advocate for restorative practices, I sure wasn't always. Back when this idea was first introduced to me in 1994, my thinking was a lot different. Restorative justice sounded like a nice little program for minor infractions, but I was sure it would never work for the serious cases I dealt with. As a police officer, it was my job to keep the community safe from serious juvenile offenders. By then, I had worked in policing for eighteen years, and I knew nothing worked to rehabilitate them—especially not this touchy-feely stuff.

My superiors sent me to a training on the philosophy of restorative justice at the University of Minnesota, and then to some practical training in victim-offender dialogue. To say that I was skeptical would be an understatement. I questioned everything—vocally. I demanded that they prove all their points to my satisfaction. I look back now and laugh about how I turned their three-day training session into a four-day exercise in defending the whole premise of restorative justice.

After I was trained, I was supposed to start taking restorative justice cases. That meant I had to actually facilitate meetings between victims, offenders, and their supporters to help them reach a resolution. I kept putting it off. Meanwhile, the other officers who had gone through the training with me were doing as they were told and coming back to the precinct with success stories. They kept talking about how often they were reaching agreements and raving about the unique process they had experienced.

Eventually, I couldn't ignore my colleagues' enthusiasm—or my boss's insistence that I take a case. So, of course, you can imagine what I did. Even though we were supposed to be working on misdemeanor property crime cases, I decided to take on an assault case, since I was eager to prove that restorative justice would never work with serious cases. This case involved two boys who had gotten into a fairly serious fight after school. Paul had been hurt pretty badly and ended up in the hospital for several days. Michael, the other boy, was charged with felony assault because of the extent of Paul's injuries. They were both fifteen or sixteen years old, as I recall. Under the juvenile court system, Michael would probably have been adjudicated delinquent and been punished—most probably put on probation with some anger management sessions included.

At first, the victim's family wasn't so crazy about being involved in a restorative justice process. But much to my chagrin, they eventually decided to try it. I completed all the preliminary meetings with everyone involved, just like I'd been trained. And then it was time for the meeting. Because they both had been fighting, we had the conference and asked both boys what happened. It was Paul, the victim, and Michael, the offender, together with both of their parents and supporters all sitting in a circle, when we began.

I was taught to start out with some open-ended questions: "What has this been like for you? What was it like when this happened? What's it been like since that time?" and then just let them talk. Paul started by explaining what the incident had been like for him. I wasn't surprised to hear it had been tough. But—can you believe it?—he also admitted that he'd egged on the kid who had hurt him. And even more surprising, he and Michael both acknowledged that Paul was a well-known bully in the community. Paul described how he sometimes felt inadequate and inferior and used bullying to cover up those feelings.

"I often feel like I'm not as good as other kids," he said. "I get told by my parents that they wish I was more like somebody else, most often Michael. I don't like it and I hate Michael for it. So I start to pick on him 'cause it makes me feel better—or at least it's supposed to."

Michael then told the group, "Paul has been picking on me for a year or more and I am tired of it. That was why I decided to put an end to it by beating him up. I had heard from teachers that the way to stop a bully was to confront them. So I did. I was tired of it and pissed off at him."

Both kids spoke about their friendship before the incident, and each one cried. These guys had known each other since they were in the second grade. Now at fifteen they were enemies involved in a serious assault. They had been good friends from the time that they were eight years old until they were about fourteen. They couldn't even say why the friendship ended, although it was clear from his earlier statement that Paul resented being compared to Michael. Things between them got worse over about a year and a half until it finally blew up.

They cried real tears, with genuine emotion behind them. The tears seemed a release from the immediate stress of this incident and also from having lost something they had both valued—their friendship. In the safe space provided by the restorative justice circle, they seemed to feel capable of allowing deep feelings to be exposed.

Paul's parents said they were surprised to hear about his feelings of inferiority and vulnerability. Michael's parents were clearly moved by Paul's story. Everyone was surprised by Paul's admission that he shared responsibility for the fight and had a role in his injuries.

I was stunned. I had never experienced this level of vulnerability or honesty in all my years in policing, and, frankly, I wasn't sure how to make sense of it. I just knew that it felt right, and it felt good. This is the dynamic of restorative justice that is simply not possible in court, where an adversarial process and the intrusion of lawyers precludes individuals from exploring their own feelings, let alone expressing them.

The participants quickly reached an agreement that ensured accountability for Michael and met everyone's needs. The agreement, too, was more thoughtful than any sentence I had ever seen from a court. The boys both agreed to go to some counseling to deal with anger and victimization. Most bullies have at some point been victims themselves, so they had to deal with that history. They wound up agreeing to go to a group counseling session together. Michael also agreed to pay for the medical bills that were still outstanding from Paul's hospital stay. Michael had $4,000 in a college fund from which he agreed to reimburse Paul's family $2,500.

They further agreed that they were going to continue talking with their parents about how and why they got to the point of physical blows, because they wanted to be friends again. They really wanted to work on that. To that end, the two families also added an agreement that called for the boys to get together one Sunday a month to share a meal. That was to go on for six months. It was significant that the families got involved in helping their kids work on restoring their past friendship. These two combatants had been friends for years, and their families were invested in seeing that relationship restored—which is why this process is called *restorative* justice. Everyone wanted to get back to a place of peaceful coexistence, and hopefully friendship. The get-togethers continued well beyond the agreement and were going strong a year later.

I can tell you that no court would ever have explored the issue of their broken friendship, and yet it was the key to preventing further violence from these young people. Had the case gone to court, a judge would have never heard from Paul, who was viewed as the victim. An attorney would have just said, "Michael beat up Paul so badly that he went to the hospital." And they would have asked Michael, "Did you do this?" Or they would have just read the charges and asked, "Do you agree with this?" And if he had said, "I did it," then that would have been it, with no further understanding of the dynamic that caused the fight or their joint culpability.

But a one-sided effort is rarely a solution.

I also doubt very much that there would have been any real positive outcome. Court is not really geared toward problem solving but instead is about a quick and clear verdict, usually involving punishment. The goal is to try and rehabilitate juveniles, but that's not really what happens. We have a very retributive kind of system focused on punishment, and that's what they can and most often do. The court might have demanded some therapy like cognitive dissonance classes—more or less demanding that the perpetrator change his thinking. Without buy-in, that sort of thing rarely works. And if both boys were not involved, the problem would have persisted. The court would also have ordered restitution and probably probation. But the root causes would not have been explored, and both boys would have likely resented the process and each other even more. But it was now clear that restoring that relationship between them was the key to ending victimization for both boys, and probably the key to preventing further violence toward others in the community.

The next day, I sought out anyone who would stand still long enough to listen to the whole story of my first circle. I raved about how remarkable, how effective, and how "right" restorative justice felt, and why we needed to commit to practicing it in our agency. Shortly after that, I was sent to a seminar in Pennsylvania for police officers on family group conferencing, which came out of Australia and is now being used in the United States.

When I returned, I immediately began practicing family group conferencing and telling everyone about all my case stories, while keeping the details confidential. I was soon assigned to coordinate the agency's community restorative justice program—mostly, I think, to get me to shut up. It didn't work. Within months, I became a trainer for the International Institute for Restorative Practices, giving presentations to other criminal justice agencies in Minnesota and beyond.

I still coordinate that program today. I also practice as a facilitator in family group conferencing and have personally handled over six hundred cases. I both practice and teach victim-offender dialogue, conferencing, and peacemaking circles.

The difference restorative justice makes to victims is obvious when you look at the research data. When we sent kids through the regular juvenile justice system, we saw a 72 percent rate of reoffending. When we started doing restorative justice, the recidivism rate for the cases that went through conferencing dropped to 18 percent. The overall recidivism rate in our jurisdiction went down to about 38 percent as a result. I call that success.

It's worked with our adults, too. I've had cases of wars between neighbors, who were tipping over swing sets and picnic tables to form barricades at their property lines. They were icing down driveways and throwing garbage on each other's lawns. When we handled these kinds of disputes through conferences and circles, those difficult discussions ended feuds and created new commitments of peace between neighbors. Annual block parties even emerged. I had one case involving arson and property damage to an elaborate tree fort. I set up a conference and had a date set, but the neighborhood got together to hold a conference before the appointed date and solved the problem on their own, which is the ultimate purpose of restorative justice: to build a community's capacity to resolve problems, foster healing, and restore relationships.

I have successfully conferenced minor criminal sexual conduct cases, many assaults, burglaries, thefts, and criminal damage cases. A community group I trained is now handling domestic abuse cases exclusively through the restorative circle process, with remarkable success. The only input from "the system" is when the prosecutor recommends a case to them. It is otherwise a completely community-driven program.

I've come a long way since that first circle. Over the course of my career in policing and public safety work, I have learned that the criminal justice system tries but regularly falls short of meeting victim's needs. It does sometimes help to hold people accountable, but it rarely makes people more reflective and committed to change. It leaves communities on the outside of the process and fails to recognize the many secondary victims impacted by what happened. The system we have is meant to punish and protect by ultimately removing offenders from society; it is not designed to restore a victim, a community, and certainly not an offender.

A criminal justice process is sometimes necessary and effective. I don't advocate that it be replaced, but rather that it incorporate restorative practices. Where restorative justice is possible, we can achieve better outcomes. When we take cases out of the court system, reach a solution that the community champions, and reduce reoffending, we save resources and money. We also salvage lives, create a more peaceful community, and empower the people to solve the problems between them on their own in a way they can embrace. *Everyone wins.*

Knowing What Is Really Needed

Pamela Purdie

Precious Blood Ministry of Reconciliation is a social services agency in Chicago that serves youth and families affected by violence. We are located in what's called the "Back of the Yards"—the former stockyards and meatpacking district that employed thousands of European immigrants in the early twentieth century. Today, the young men the ministry serves are fourteen to twenty-six years old. It's hard for boys in this neighborhood to "come up" without having a record, and most have been in gangs or in some kind of trouble.

We run several programs that help young men with job readiness and older men returning from prison with reentry supports, as well as programs for young women and for mothers who have lost their sons to gun violence. Everything we do is based on restorative justice; we offer peacemaking circles on Saturdays as part of every program. My job is to help the staff and youth understand restorative justice and what it means in everything that we do. By using restorative justice practices, we create a place that is safe.

I met Shanna Swanson, a stalwart volunteer at our agency, soon after I started at Precious Blood Ministry. She had been a friend of the program for a long time. Even though we receive help from a local food pantry and other places, Shanna often brought groceries and other needed supplies for us. She also shopped for things we needed, like shoes for our kids.

One day, Shanna had been shopping and was bringing quite a few things inside. Sister Donna and another one of our program participants were helping her carry groceries from her car. After they had finished putting everything away, Sister Donna, Shanna, and Shanna's friend decided to go out for lunch. Shanna knew she'd had money in her purse earlier, so when she went to pay the bill, she was surprised to find that almost $200 in cash was missing! She suspected what might have happened to it. When they returned, she approached Julian, one of the young men who had helped bring things in. She asked him if he had taken the money. He denied it, but Shanna knew he was the only person who could have stolen it.

I was so angry when I heard about the incident. I thought, *How could you do that when she is such a good person and comes here all the time and brings things to us? How could you?* The whole idea of some-one stealing from such a generous person was shocking. It made for a very difficult time, and at first Shanna didn't want to come back to the ministry. Father Denny, who had been a mentor to Julian and was trying to help him get a job and an apartment, talked to Shanna about returning, but she just didn't feel comfortable.

Some time went by before Julian finally admitted to Father Denny that he had taken $195 from Shanna's wallet. Julian told Father Denny that he wanted to make it right, because he knew he'd really done something wrong. The worst part, he knew, was that Shanna didn't want to come back to Precious Blood anymore. He was familiar with the peacemaking circles at Precious Blood and asked if he could be in a circle with Shanna so he could apologize. Shanna agreed, and Father Denny asked me to facilitate the circle.

The circle keeper always interviews everyone who will be in the circle before it starts. I interviewed Julian about what he wanted from the circle, since he had been the one to ask for it. He said, "Father Denny told me Shanna isn't coming here anymore. I want to get in the circle with Shanna and let her know, first of all, that I'm sorry and that I feel bad because she's not coming back to the center." I asked who else he wanted to have in the circle. He wanted to include Father Denny, because he was his mentor, and Father

Kelly, because Julian sensed that Father Kelly had been treating him differently since he stole the money. Julian wanted to make things right with him as well. Julian also wanted to include Sister Donna and two other people who worked at Precious Blood. When I interviewed Shanna, she said she would like to include her friend who was with her at the restaurant when she discovered the money had been stolen.

We gathered for the circle.

First, I asked everyone to think of important people in their life. I asked who they would like to make the world safe for and had them write down their names. Next, I asked them to name the people they had in their lives to support them. Then, I asked who they admired. We went around the circle and spoke about the names we had written down, and I noticed Julian didn't have a long list, but when he talked about his son, he lit up.

We talked about how we hope people will treat us, and how we treat others when we're on our best behavior. We named our shared values, which included honesty, trust, respect, and listening. We wrote these down and put them in the middle of the circle. We talked about how we would try to live by those values during our circle.

We were then ready to start talking about the harm. I turned to Shanna first and asked what she was hoping for from this circle. She said that mostly she wanted to know: Why the theft? Why would Julian want to steal from her? Shanna wanted him to know how much it had meant to her to volunteer there, and how much she was missing it. She hesitated a moment and then added that she wanted to tell him how upset she was that he didn't admit it right away, and that it took him so long to do so.

Julian apologized. He explained that he was a diabetic and had really needed money that day to pick up the medicine he needed.

He said he hadn't been getting his medicine the way he was sup-posed to and had been feeling awful lately. But, he added, he had also wanted to get something for his young son's birthday. So part of the money went to that, too.

Several others in the circle asked Julian why he hadn't gone to Father Kelly or Father Denny or someone else for help instead of stealing. Jonathan, another employee of Precious Blood Ministry who mentors some of our boys, admitted that he had backed away from being Julian's mentor after the theft. Others in the circle said how disappointed they had been in Julian.

Julian's head was down as he apologized again, telling Shanna how sorry he was, and how he now understood that it was a huge mistake. He said he knew that both Fathers Kelly and Denny also felt differently about him now. He said, "I want you to know that I hear all the things you try to say to me to help me. I hear and I understand." The worst thing, he said, was knowing how he had let everyone down. He wanted to find a way to make it up to Shanna and everyone else, including by paying back every cent of the money he'd stolen. He said, "I need you to see me as the person I am today and to know that I will continue to grow into the person you want me to be."

He went around the circle, addressing each person by name and genuinely apologizing to them. And then, he asked Shanna and the rest of the group what he could do to make up for what he had done.

The reason this story still sticks with me is what happened next. When we asked Shanna, "Now that you have heard everything that has been said, what is it that *you* want and how can we support you?" she turned to Julian and said, "I just want you to realize what you did was terrible. But, also, I don't want you ever to not have money for your medicine. Or for your son."

She asked Julian if she could mentor him, and if he would agree to check in with her once or twice a month just to let her know how he was doing. She also said she didn't want him to have to pay the money back.

I'm telling you, from then on it was just amazing! She would always check on him and he would always check in with her. She made sure he had enough money for his medicine. He didn't get into trouble anymore—no arguments, no fights. Precious Blood helped Julian find an apartment and he was able to get a job. He and his girlfriend got married and have three children now. They moved out of the Back of the Yards, and Julian is doing well in a construction job that allows him to support his family. Although Julian is no longer receiving services from Precious Blood, he and Father Denny are still good friends. One recent January, Father Kelly and Father Denny did the polar plunge in Lake Michigan. Julian and his wife and newest baby were there to participate, raising funds for Precious Blood. Shanna sponsored the whole family. It was great to see how well he's doing.

At Precious Blood, we talk about how the best part of peacemaking circles is that they create a space for people to do the right thing. If Shanna had called the police, Julian would have been charged, arrested, and forced to sit in jail until his court date. He may have been locked up and kept from his son for a long time. We have a decision to make with young people who get in trouble. We can banish them from our communities, which gives them no way to repair the harm they caused. Or we can offer a safe space to hear about their needs, explain what people need from them, and then help them make it right.

When I think back on that circle, I think of how powerful it was for me, too. When I asked each of them what they wanted from the circle, I had no idea it would end up catalyzing powerful, life-changing relationships. In my experience, circles are a way to meet people's real needs. Sometimes, all a person wants is a heartfelt apology. Sometimes it's having the person who harmed them not only apologize but also fix it. Often, it's reassurance that the situation will never happen again. Restorative justice does not mean that the offender gets away with something. When we have a safe place to talk about what happened, we usually find out what is behind their behavior. Maybe a bad relationship between a young girl and her mother that has made her angry. But you would not know this unless we created a space where there is honesty. In these spaces we find out what everyone's needs are, so that those who have done wrong can be held accountable for the harm they have caused.

When Julian called the circle, he wanted more than to be held accountable. He did not want to be known only for the mistake he had made; he wanted Shanna to get to know the better person he was becoming. And that's what happened in the two years after that circle. They created a relationship that has blossomed into a friendship.

Recently, Shanna was diagnosed with a malignant brain tumor. Julian still visits her with Father Denny. He goes to see her because she touched him so deeply, and he thinks the world of her. Shanna is now in hospice and is expected to pass away soon. Even now, when she is unable to speak, she and Julian are still very close. She told Father Denny that she and her husband have put just enough money in her will for Julian to make sure he has enough for his medicine for the rest of his life.

Julian will grow older and wiser, knowing that he has become the kind of person Shanna can be proud of. Although Precious Blood helped him a lot (it even bought him boots when he got his job), it was Julian who worked the hardest to put himself on a successful path. Sometimes all it takes is for someone to show they care about and believe in them to get them started on that journey.

Building Relationships Doesn't Happen in Court

Jane Otte

Many years ago, when people had only landline phones, I helped with a conference for two kids. They were so young—just ten and thirteen. These two boys were in a group that had pulled the phone junction box off a senior housing building, disrupting phone service for everyone who lived there. They had also stolen lawn equipment from an elderly woman, Mrs. Armstrong. They'd been asked to be part of a family group conference to address what they'd done. The boys were reluctant at first, because they didn't want to admit guilt, and the conference was a new and scary thing. But the alternative for the boys was to go through the juvenile probation system, and that didn't sound good to them either.

For me, the best part of the restorative justice process is the element of surprise. Every time I'm either facilitating a conference or sitting in on one, something happens that I would never expect. Every time!

I came early to the meeting place that night. Mrs. Armstrong was there early, too. You know how it is with older folks—they don't like to be late. Mrs. Armstrong talked to me while we waited. She asked if she could share some letters that she had brought with her from her grandson. I must have looked at her quizzically, because she said, "My grandson is in prison, and I want the boys to know that this could happen to them if they do things like this." She gripped those letters like they were all she had from her grandson. They probably were. My heart went out to her. Then she shook her head sadly. "You know, I really don't understand why they couldn't have just talked to me instead of taking the lawn equipment. They could have just asked me to loan them some of those things. I'm not a scary person."

After a pause, she went on. "I *am* glad to be here, but I'm worried about driving home in the dark."

Slowly, others arrived and helped arrange chairs in a circle. One of the boys was with his mom and sister, and one of the boys was with his dad. The director of the senior housing facility then arrived, as did a probation officer and two community members who were employees from a local college.

It was obvious that they were all uncomfortable, except Mrs. Armstrong. She knew what she wanted to say. Everyone else in the circle was a stranger to the others, and they had been brought together under unfortunate circumstances. You could tell this was all new to them. The boys looked at the floor while the director of the senior housing facility glared at them. Mrs. Armstrong just sat with her hands on those letters, calm as you please.

To begin the process, the boys spoke about the day they had damaged the property. I could tell they were scared to be sitting there. I could see it in their body language—no eye contact, soft voices, few words. Very succinctly, they admitted to the theft and damage. Both parents were visibly upset and embarrassed. Even the boy's sister seemed frustrated and recounted another recent incident when she had been looking after her brother while her mom was away and he started acting up. She said she wished he would straighten up.

The director of the senior housing facility was angry. She said that when the phone system was pulled off the building, it left them without any phone service at all. If anything had happened to their elderly residents during that time, they could not have called for help. I looked around the room and saw the looks on the boys' faces as they realized how their stupid prank could have caused real harm.

It was finally Mrs. Armstrong's turn to speak. In a soft voice, she shared that the lawn equipment had been a gift to her late husband, and what that meant to her. Then she added, "I really don't want you boys to end up where my grandson is—in prison." When she said that, you could hear a pin drop. She proceeded to read one of the letters from her grandson.

Following that, both boys really apologized. Their heads were down, their hands were fidgety, and they spoke softly. Each of them looked at Mrs. Armstrong and said there was no excuse for their behavior, and that they were ashamed.

As the evening went on, the director of the senior housing facility asked the boys many questions. I noticed that she became more and more curious about them, asking what they were interested in at school and whether they had any hobbies. After learning one of the boys was an aspiring artist, she encouraged him to keep practicing, and even asked if he could show her his work the next time they met.

In the end, it seemed to me that the contract everyone agreed upon was harsher than a probation sanction might have been. The boys had to make a public apology to the senior housing board, help pay for the lawn equipment, and visit Mrs. Armstrong every other Saturday. The boys were going to visit the person they'd harmed every other week; can you imagine? I was all in favor of the agreement—I was part of it, after all, since all conference outcomes are by consensus. But it sure reminded me that being held accountable to others in our community often requires a lot more of us than the punishments doled out by the justice system. Since then, I've also often thought about how this conference ended up bringing more caring adults into these boys' lives.

Oh—and the surprise! As Mrs. Armstrong and I were talking at the end of the evening, I asked whether she felt okay about driving home. One of the boys' parents overheard, and said, "Hey, I don't live far from you. We can follow you back to make sure you get home safe."

Before I discovered restorative justice, I never expected that a harmful incident like this could lead to new community relationships, but it did. I'll bet *that* never happens in a courtroom.

From Boys to Men

Terri Masiello

My story begins with an African Methodist Episcopal Zion Church in my rural South community. The congregation had just finished building a new sanctuary next door to their old one and had recently begun worshiping in the new building. Their plan was to renovate the old sanctuary so that they could rent it to another church that was interested in it. The rent would assist with the construction costs of their new place of worship.

One Saturday when members arrived at the site, they found the old sanctuary in shambles. A window in the back had been smashed, and inside they found their stained-glass windows shattered, the lights in smithereens, much of the drywall destroyed, and their dishes in pieces everywhere. It was a devastating mess.

The police were called. They looked through the church's exterior camera footage to find that four white male juveniles had smashed through the back window and entered. They had arrived and later left on their bicycles. While there, they had caused over $20,000 in damage. It was easy to see who the offenders were. Even though juveniles' records are confidential, these white youth were well known in the community, and the peaceful town quickly became rife with racial tension and accusations. The local paper had pictures of the damage, and the local radio station held a day of "comments" on air. There were letters to the editors and malicious gossip. Rancor in the community was escalating.

I was the executive director at our multicounty restorative justice center when we received a diversion referral from Juvenile Justice for three of the young boys. We later learned there was a fourth who was heading to juvenile court because of his prior run-ins with police. The boys ranged in age from thirteen to fifteen, with the oldest being the youth with the prior police encounter. When we learned that there were actually four offenders, we began working toward bringing that fourth youth in as well.

We started by interviewing the boys and their parents. We learned that the boys had been riding their bicycles around town that Friday. They saw the empty sanctuary and broke in through a window in the back. One thing led to another, and they had a rip-roaring good time. They rode their bicycles up the walls, destroyed windows and stained glass. They took the plates and used them like frisbees across the room. The physical damage was extensive.

The psychic damage was considerable, too. The community was inflamed over what seemed like an all-too-familiar hate crime: four white boys tearing up a Black church in a Southern community. We then reached out to the church elders to discuss a restorative justice victim-offender conference.

The six church elders who spoke with us were understandably very angry and wanted to prosecute the boys to the full extent of the law. We chose our youth director, who is incredibly skilled at speaking about restorative practices, to confer with the elders. As a fellow Christian, she was able to discuss candidly what outcomes could be positive for the church in handling this situation.

Our youth director reassured the elders that restorative justice prioritizes the needs of those victimized. "This is a way for you to not only find some healing for your church, but also for the entire community. It will help to hold the youths accountable and have an impact on them as well. If you don't like what's happening at any point, you can stop, and you can walk away." The elders were skeptical but said they would be willing to try a victim-offender conference.

In the preconferencing meetings we held first with the boys and their parents, the boys were scared that this was going to impact their lives for a very long time. None of them wanted to be labeled criminals. The three had not been in trouble before—no suspensions, no run-ins with the police. And even though the fourth boy had a previous police offense, it had not become a court case. During our meetings we explained that we were recommending they meet with the elders for a restorative justice conference, and that this would be a good opportunity for them to make things right with the church to the best of their ability and to avoid a prosecution in juvenile court.

We decided we would follow our traditional format of questions for the boys: What happened? What were you thinking at the time you were doing it? What have you thought about since? Who do you think was impacted? What was the real harm that was done? What needs to be done to repair the harm? We suggested the boys give thought to their answers before we met. After meetings with the elders, the youth and their parents, and the defense attorney for the young man in juvenile court, we scheduled a restorative conference at the new church sanctuary.

The boys were very scared and didn't want to tattle on each other. It was hard to get them to state who did what. Did one person peer-pressure the others into it? We asked a lot about that. It seemed like they all were a part of it. There was no ringleader.

It became clear in the conversation that none of them had any history with that building or any of the church members. Nor had it occurred to them that trashing the building might get them in trouble; they were just bored, and they thought no one would care because it appeared to them to be an old, abandoned building. And, typical of boys with young brains, they also didn't think about getting caught. They just figured they'd ride away. They never considered that there might be a surveillance camera.

Then it was time to discuss "What have you thought about since that time? What are you thinking now?" They were now aware that what they'd done was serious, and that the entire town had reacted, given the long, ugly history of violent attacks on Black churches in the South. They were able to express how sorry they were for what they had done. But when giving their accounts, none of the boys could look directly at the harmed parties; instead, they looked at the floor or glanced around the room nervously. The youngest of the boys was the most reticent. He kept looking at his father, as if for permission, before giving his story. The fifteen-year-old, meanwhile, had the most confidence and was able to explain that they had entered and damaged the sanctuary because they were bored and thought it would be fun to tear things up. He also articulated his remorse, saying that he appreciated the chance to have this meeting and hoped he could share it with the judge at his future court date, in case it might make a difference in how he was sentenced.

Most of the parents were very angry with their boys and had put in place a lot of restrictions on them. But there was one father who minimized their actions and took the view that they were being unduly condemned. When his son was talking about what had happened, the father kept interjecting, saying, "Why are we making such a big deal out of this? These are just boys. Boys do this kind of stuff. Boys get in trouble." He felt the community's reaction was extreme, and he worried for his son's safety.

We explained to him that "We'll give you an opportunity to talk, but we need to let your son talk for himself right now." As the son was talking, he kept looking at his father, as if asking, "How much do I say? What do I say?"

Then it was the time for the elders to speak. They shared how the trashing of their longtime sanctuary was emotionally scarring. It was sacred space. And then there were the extreme emotions of fear and anger, based on their assumption that the boys' actions were racially motivated. The damage also had a big financial impact, because they were counting on renting the old sanctuary as a source of revenue to finance their new building.

But as angry as they had been, they released that anger after meeting the boys and their parents. They heard genuine remorse and a commitment from the boys to make it right. They understood that the way to make an impact on these youth was not to beat them over the head, but to reach their hearts. The elders said, "We want you to grow from this. We want you to learn. We want you to understand how your behaviors impact others. We want you to be better men than this." We could begin to see empathy and reconciliation.

After the father heard these sentiments from the church elders, he, too, changed his position. He now understood how much the boys' actions had impacted the church, both emotionally and financially, and why it had caused such uproar within the community. He was really able to hear what the elders said, in part because they expressed themselves in a way that was kind and not critical. He was expecting them to attack his son, but they didn't. They spoke honestly about their pain and hardship, but they did not condemn the boys. He said, "My son and I are here to make this right." He even apologized for not knowing what his son was doing on that day.

All the parents agreed on a multifaceted plan for repairing the harm the boys had done. First of all, each of the boys had to pay $200 in the form of forty hours of community service credited at $5 an hour (although some of them did more than that). Typically, our community service is at a nonprofit or the local soup kitchen, but all their community service was to be done at the church.

All four boys also took a four-hour Building Peace course, held at the restorative justice center in our county, that teaches about

assertive versus aggressive language, anger management and conflict resolution, empathy, and other skill-building tools.

Even though the boys apologized during the conference, the
elders wanted them to apologize to the entire congregation as well.
The boys all wrote letters of apology to the church. Since they
were juveniles, their names were left off so the letters could be cir-
culated around the church.

In order to complete their forty hours of community service, the
youths and parents joined the church elders and members of the
congregation for four weekends of demolition, cleanup, trips to the
dump, purchase of repair supplies, and repair work. The parents
brought in flatbed trailers for trips to the dump. The youth worked
side by side with those same elders they had conferenced with and
other church members, but also with construction workers. They
learned how to use a hammer and screwdriver, install a window, put
up drywall, and paint walls. Because it was a construction site and
there was a lot of broken glass around, their parents were always
there with them, supervising. In fact, the father who was initially
resistant participated the most of all of them. He paid for the fees
at the dump and made sure his son attended every opportunity to
assist the church.

When the repairs were done, the church invited the boys and
their families to a blessing ceremony at the old sanctuary. It was an
intimate event—just the people who were involved in the conference and a few others. The church called each of the youths' families personally to invite them to the blessing. There were tables
with tablecloths and light refreshments, and floral arrangements
graced the sanctuary. The minister spoke for ten minutes or so
about the efforts of the boys and their families, the reconciliation felt by the church members, and the way that God used this
moment to heal a community and to make it stronger.

The church elders also invited the boys to come to the new sanctuary whenever they wanted to, whether to become a part of the congregation or just to drop in and visit. Even though some people were still upset about what had happened, the boys' destructive act faded with time. Many people in the community saw the work they did to repair the old sanctuary, and how the congregation had chosen to embrace the better men these boys could still become. I believe that none of this true reconciliation would have been possible without the understanding that a restorative dialogue brought forth.

4.
Understanding the Cause of Offenses

Restorative conversations often open a window into the life events that contribute to youthful offending. When implemented in a trauma-informed manner, restorative processes both reveal and acknowledge the impact of home or other adverse circumstances on a young person's behavior—not to excuse the behavior, but to determine how best to respond to the youth's needs and prevent a recurrence. The stories in this chapter illustrate how juvenile justice stakeholders can use restorative justice to address behavioral health while also preserving public safety.

Changing the World
One Conversation at a Time

Eric Butler

I am a survivor of Hurricane Katrina. After leaving New Orleans and moving to Oakland, California, I knew that I wanted to work with youth and adults around experiences of trauma. I took a position with a project of Catholic Charities called Crisis Response. We would go to murder scenes and then work to address the repercussions of violence and trauma on the people directly impacted. I found myself working with elementary, middle, and high school children using a circle format before I was ever actually trained to facilitate such meetings. We would sit in circle to talk about what happened when they had witnessed violence.

I later joined Restorative Justice for Oakland Youth as the nation's first in-school restorative justice coordinator. I was assigned to the Ralph J. Bunche Continuation High School. In California, a "continuation high school" is a last-chance school, populated with young people who were expelled or near expulsion and who are at risk of not graduating on time. Many of these young people are entangled with the justice system. I knew that misbehavior was a symptom of a deeper issue, and I found early on that circles were an important route to addressing those root causes.

The principal of Ralph J. Bunche Continuation High School, Betsey Steele, was an active participant in what is now known as the school-to-prison pipeline. She was a veteran principal who, when I first met her, described herself proudly as the "Queen of Suspensions." She would continue to discipline any student who came to her office in the same way she'd always dealt with them. She knew this went against everything that I believed in and had been working against, but she was intentionally establishing that she was in charge.

I knew that my first step, and a critical one, was to develop a relationship with Ms. Steele. I initiated one-on-one conversations to find out what she liked and what we had in common. I tried to figure out how she could hear me when it came to restorative versus punitive approaches to discipline. After many conversations and intentional relationship building, we became friends, and she started to listen to and understand the theory of restorative justice. She realized that the whole time she'd been in education, she'd been doing it wrong.

After we worked together for a while, she decided that whenever new students came to the school, she wouldn't look at their disciplinary records. She didn't want their past experiences to bias her against them. We were starting something brand new with restorative justice, and she was a big part of it.

One day a young boy named Cedric came to our school from juvenile hall. Students often returned to Bunche after being suspended or expelled from another school or incarcerated, and this was his case. Instead of processing Cedric the old way, Ms. Steele and I invited him to what is typically termed a "reintegration" circle. But since Cedric was coming to Bunche for the first time, we called it a "welcoming" circle. I was responsible for prepping the welcoming process with Cedric. While doing so, I noticed that he was shy and hesitant to tell me what had actually happened to result in his incarceration. I'm assuming he didn't want to be recharged with the crime. That was his experience as a fifteen-year-old Black boy; once you knew about something bad that he had done, that's who he became to you.

But after a few days of getting to know each other, we were able to build our relationship. He began to open up. The thing is, kids won't open up if we don't take the time to build trust. So this is what I did first. Reluctantly he told me that his mother had been on and off drugs for a long time. It happened so often that his family knew when she would relapse. He and his siblings even had a name for it. They would call it "hungry time."

When he said that, my ears perked up. I wanted to know why he called it hungry time, although I had an idea. Cedric explained that when his mother relapsed, there would be little food for him and his siblings, and they often would go nights without eating. At fifteen, Cedric was the oldest kid in the house. He committed to finding a way to solve their chronic hunger. He didn't see any other options at the time, and it was urgent.

He knew a drug dealer in his neighborhood. They weren't friends, but Cedric was hopeful the dealer might lend him some money. The thought of going to this dealer was a no-brainer. The drug dealer told Cedric that he would not give him anything, but that he could work to make money to get the things that he needed for his family.

Cedric did not know how to sell drugs. He was bad at it. In fact, he was so bad that the first day he tried, somebody robbed him of the package he had to sell. Now he had to go back to the drug dealer and tell him that he didn't have the money, and he didn't have the drugs.

Now, I've never sold drugs. But I lived in drug-infested neighborhoods when I was young, and I can imagine the terror that Cedric faced having to deliver the drug dealer this news. But instead of whatever terrible thing he expected would happen, the drug dealer embraced him and laughed. Can you imagine Cedric's surprise at receiving a hug?

This neighborhood drug dealer then gave Cedric a lesson in street-smart pharmaceutical representation. He handed Cedric a gun and told him to use it to protect their investment. He was *not* to use the gun to shoot anybody, he said, but absolutely to intimidate someone if necessary.

So every day, Cedric would go to school with his gun in his backpack and drugs in his pocket to sell on his way home. One day he took his backpack off in the classroom, and the gun went off. No one was hurt, thankfully, but the police were called to the school. Cedric was arrested and went to the juvenile detention center for ten months. In Oakland, depending on what you've done, the school has the right to say whether they'll take you back if you went to jail. Cedric's school said he couldn't come back. He would have to go to a continuation school.

At the time, Oakland had four continuation schools, and even those schools didn't have to take you. And if they didn't, you'd end up going to an adult school from which you were almost sure not to graduate. Ms. Steele and I had already agreed that we'd take any kid that wanted to come to Bunche. Cedric had confided his story to me, but Ms. Steele didn't know anything about the circumstances of his arrest. And now my responsibility was to prep folks on staff to be able to support Cedric. Fortunately, by that time Ms. Steele and I had already built a lot of relationships within the school that supported the use of restorative justice.

Restorative justice in school settings is sometimes thought of in three tiers. First is community building, where adults and youth together have intentional conversations about what will work best to help them feel safe within the school system. Building relationships with students and teachers as well as other staff is an important foundation for actual restorative processes to take root and shift the school's culture. And building relationships requires slowing down, a willingness to be vulnerable as an adult, and modeling the same to others. When this step is skipped, it leads to failures down the road.

Harm and conflict support is the stage needed when harm occurs in the school community. Staff and students, along with the responsible youth, work together both to hold the youth accountable for the harm caused and to co-create ideas for repairing the harm.

Intensive support circles deal with students who are grieving a loss or have been out of school due to suspensions or expulsion. With the help of restorative justice processes, these students are given a chance to be welcomed back into the school community.

Our goal with Cedric was reintegration to a school community, even though he was attending Bunche High School for the first time. The day of his welcoming circle arrived. Cedric had been in foster care for a while, and his foster parent, who had worked in West Oakland with other kids in similar circumstances, was there participating. His caseworker was also there. I knew both of them.

A total of fourteen people were in the circle: Cedric, his biological mom, his foster mom, his stepdad, his lawyer, his caseworker, Ms. Steele, the assistant principal, the school attendance clerk, the school psychologist, the school discipline specialist, a placement specialist, another student, and me. I knew almost all of them except Cedric's biological mom and stepdad.

It was my responsibility to prep everyone. It was important that they each knew that we were not investigating a crime or retrying Cedric; he had already been punished. This circle was about welcoming Cedric into school by helping him understand what was expected of him and helping us understand what he needed to be successful. This included getting him caught up on the things that he had missed from the previous year. It was also a way to shine light on Cedric's community of support as each person in the circle had a chance to share their belief in him, and what they saw in him. This shifted the energy in the room to a depth that helped us then make decisions about actions.

Days after the circle was over, Cedric told me how he felt when it started. He said, "All eyes were on me, my hands were sweating. I was really nervous—my mom and my stepdad were there. It made me feel like just walking out the damn door. That is really what it felt like: Let's just cancel this. It was too much tension."

When a kid initially doesn't want to be in a restorative justice circle, it is understandable. It's hard to trust a new process when they believe that they can't trust anyone there. We knew we had a lot of relationship building to do, but I was also excited to show everyone in the circle how to get from here to there and go beyond.

We began by explaining that we use a talking piece. We asked everyone if they have ever felt that no one was listening when they were talking. We explained that when you have the talking piece everyone is listening to you. They aren't thinking about what they want to say next. They will have their turn. And then you will have your turn to listen to others.

Our first rounds in a circle are for introductions and relationship building. In our circle with Cedric, we began by asking, "What did you want to be when you were a kid?" We went around the room.

"I wanted to work with kids."

"My main thing was I wanted to be a cosmetologist."

"I wanted to be a race car driver."

"When I was a kid, I wanted to be a preacher."

"When I was a little girl, I wanted to be a singer."

"I wanted to make my community better."

"I wanted to be a healer."

"I just wanted to be happy . . . and I am."

When it got to Cedric, we were all waiting for him to respond. Finally he said, "I wanted to play football."

Turns out we are all pretty much the same.

Next it was time for our values round. We asked what the values were that would help us feel safe and comfortable as we talked together. Responses were typical of what most of us hope for in a circle: Commitment. Respect. Always speak your truth. Compassion. Honesty. Forgiveness. Staying connected. Integrity. Sensitivity.

Later, Cedric told me that is when he started to realize that "they weren't there to stereotype me, but to help me. They were trying to see what was going on in my head. So I straightened up a little."

Next came the needs and responsibilities discussion rounds. Cedric heard what pledges the members of the circle were making to him:

"I'm the person you can always count on." (Cedric's biological mother)

"I'm the person you can always come to." (Cedric's stepfather)

"I'm the person who is going to love you to death." (School discipline specialist)

"I'm the person who is going to make sure you earn your high school diploma and get on with your life." (Ms. Steele)

"I'm the person who is going to remind you that you can be the person you want to be." (Vice Principal Lorna Shelton)

Later Cedric said to me, "That touched me and made me feel like I could do it. At first, I didn't trust them, but then as they kept talking and looking me in the eye and telling me what they could do, I thought, *Yeah, maybe I can give them a chance and maybe I can do this.*"

We knew he would need the support that we promised him. We told him:

"We need you to be open and fearless."

"This road to your success is going to be tough."

"I will walk through the fire with you. I'm with you, but I am not you."

We explained that we needed him to have the most confidence

in the world. That no one can tell you that your education doesn't come first.

There had never been a time in Cedric's life when everyone in his school was so concerned about his well-being. He was the entire focus of that circle. Most probably he had never been the main focus of anything before.

His biological mom said, "When you need to talk to somebody and you need that confidence and you need to call someone, you call me anytime."

His stepdad said, "I want you to grow to be the man you want to follow—that's what I need from you."

Cedric said, "I never listened to my mom like that before. I was like, I guess I need to talk to my stepdad more, 'cause I know I just do whatever I want. It's not like I was peer-pressured to do all the stuff I was doing. I just need to keep myself motivated. Because I know I can do it. I just haven't been motivated."

Finally, I said, "Everybody in this room has your back. I know that you carry a heavy load sometimes because you worry about your family. I know that! And I worry about you worrying about your family. I think some of the reasons you made the decisions in your life are because of your worry about your family. When there is something in the way, you need to tell us, so we know how to help you.

"What I need from you is to keep coming back to the circle. Bring your successes to the circle to share with others. Bring your challenges back to the circle so we can keep helping you."

It was time to develop our plan.

In the circle, we came up with a plan where everybody had a responsibility in creating a vehicle of success for Cedric. For example, some suggested the possibility of having a tutor or help in finding him an internship as time went by. And that's what happened.

Cedric ended up graduating with a 3.8 GPA. I remember that so well because throughout the year we talked, and he kept saying that he had never experienced having good grades before. And the reason he thought he was doing so well was because he had support and had finally been heard. It was a community effort to help get Cedric through high school.

After high school, he went to community college and then transferred to the University of California, Berkeley. The last time I heard from Cedric, he owned his own construction business. He was doing quite well.

The reason this story is so important is because that was not his original trajectory. Usually when we hear about kids that start off with suspensions and stints in juvenile detention, they end up in jail again and suffering a worse fate. I think Cedric was able to escape that outcome because the people in the circle committed to doing things differently. So often we throw these kids to the wayside. I know that when kids have an ankle monitor on, they're treated differently. I've worked at schools where school resource officers were frisking kids at the door without even saying "Good morning."

Schools should be a place to experience a high level of humanity. But instead of his original school providing that, Cedric got a humane response from someone whom society deems to be the worst part of our communities: a drug dealer, who hugged him instead of hurting him when he was robbed. Unfortunately, it was only after his prosecution and yearlong incarceration that Cedric—thanks to the restorative practice of community reintegration—received the kind of support that was able to identify the root cause of his behaviors and guide him to successful adulthood.

From Victim to Offender to Facilitator

Eva Vega

Restorative justice is often thought of as a journey of learning, changing, and healing rather than simply an act of punishment meant to eliminate wrongdoing. My story is of my journey of learning, changing, and healing which ironically has found me right where I started.

I would like to start by telling you about me and how I grew up. My Papi, an immigrant from Mexico, was twenty-four and my mom was fourteen when they met. He beat her a lot and I know she left him because of the abuse. But then he found her and brought her back. He was an alcoholic and a pretty serious paranoid schizophrenic. And he kept beating her. I am the youngest of three girls. After my siblings and I were born, he beat all of us.

Finally, when I was nine, my mom left him for good. But then she brought home this gang-affiliated guy she met in California. He was a pedophile, so as soon as he arrived, he was sexually assaulting and sodomizing my sisters and me. That lasted for four years. My eldest sister was reporting the physical and sexual abuse a lot. But I always lied about it. I was scared to tell the truth, and at that age, when that happens to you, you mostly think you are doing something wrong.

And then when I was thirteen, the police and child welfare came to my school and took me. I had ten minutes to grab my stuff. I was completely traumatized when I was taken from my mom.

I was both sexually and physically abused at foster care. I was really angry. It is difficult to share all the trouble we had. When we were in foster care, I had to testify about the abuse there in a courtroom. That was so difficult. My life was a mess. I guess you could say that I looked to the streets to find love or to find that camaraderie and that belonging feeling that I never had.

I was getting into a lot of trouble and was suspended from school several times. I was stealing—mostly clothes and necessities. But then, I also started to steal cigarettes or alcohol, obviously things I didn't need. I got caught stealing several times and taken to juvenile court. But whenever I got into trouble, it seemed the judge was familiar with stuff that my siblings and I were experiencing as children, and I was never locked up at any kind of detention. So in a lot of ways, you could say I was getting by with a lot of stuff.

I was getting into a lot of fights. I continued to be very violent. One time when I was fighting, the teacher tried to break us apart. I ended up assaulting the teacher. And to this day, I don't have a recollection of it, but I know that that's what they said, and that's what the witnesses there said. And so I was expelled. I wasn't allowed to come back for the rest of the year. I had to go to an anger management school. I spent my eighth grade at that school. I remember I was fourteen then and had to do a lot of community service that year. But also, a lot of that was a blur because I was going through so much trauma, and I was drinking a lot. I was stealing cars, too, but never got caught for doing that.

When I was sixteen, I refused to go to foster care. A boyfriend who was selling drugs helped me to run away. I had become a ward of the court. There were many times when I got in trouble and ended up having to do community service instead of jail time. There were many times when I was handcuffed, put in the police car, and then let go, even though I had become a very violent person. I wasn't living on the street, thank God, because I know so many people who do. But I would go from home to home, different people's houses, couch surfing. I didn't have a place to call home.

That's what I knew. I caused a lot of harm in my community.

I remember, I had charges for damaging a Tri-Met public transportation bus. I had gotten in a fight, and I punched hard enough to break the window. That is when I went to Rosemary Anderson Prep School in Portland. I wasn't court-ordered there, but the court just told me I had to go to school.

I was still sixteen when I first went to Rosemary Anderson. Dr. Anderson was a Black woman who founded the school in the mid-1980s. She saw that Black people in the community here in Portland needed help, especially with education, since a lot of Black kids were getting kicked out of school. For the first time, I had adults around me that cared about me. And I had access to opportunities I never had before—instruction on writing a résumé, training on job skills and computer literacy, all of these things I didn't know. They trained me, they taught me, and then they gave me a paid internship so I didn't need to go out to find a man to hustle, because I was making my own money legally.

When I first arrived at Rosemary Anderson, it happened that they were already using culturally specific practices that were rooted in Afro-Indigenous restorative justice. Back when I came to the school in the mid-nineties, it had already been around for about a decade. I was one of three students who were not Black. I didn't know that the practices they were using were based on restorative dialogue; I learned that later. Those were early days of using trauma-informed care with young people and it fit with the restorative justice practices they were built on. It was and still is a part of the school's organizational policy.

One thing that makes it a little different, too, and probably worth mentioning, is that Rosemary Anderson was one of the schools that contracted with the Youth Opportunity Center, known as the YO Center. They were doing restorative work there, too, such as peacemaking circles and other restorative practices. The mentors, the people that I had at the school, were serving me also at the YO Center. And that's where I first encountered circles for community healing and conflict resolution.

I was having a problem with three other students. These girls were saying things about me that made me really upset, and I wanted to fight them. One of the school staff members said they were going to have us talk about what was going on. I didn't know what they meant by that. It was my first experience with a circle. There were four of us and two staff people. The staff provided the structure. They set the stage to talk about the harm that was done and reconciliation.

They brought us into this room with the chairs all set up in a circle. They had a centerpiece in the middle, and they gave us a talking piece and explained the ground rules—for example, that you don't talk unless you have the talking piece, and you respect the speaker. I didn't think it was going to be effective. It initially felt very unsafe. I didn't want to be vulnerable or share out. I was resistant because I was used to just dealing with things by using violence. I didn't know about using my voice to communicate, especially with conflict. But hearing other people be able to do it made me feel like I could, too.

The staff modeled for us what it meant to have a respectful dialogue with conflict, to have meaningful conversations where everyone was heard. And to have a conversation with the outcome not being that you need to do specific things to make up for what you did wrong, but that you work it out together.

And it created this closeness with what felt like were my opponents. We didn't get along, we wanted to fight each other, and suddenly we were connecting. And that tension wasn't there.

I began to realize I had to really exercise the discipline of not speaking out of turn and practice being a good listener—listening to understand, instead of listening to respond. And it made me realize that sometimes my perceptions of people's intentions weren't true. That was hard for me at the time. It was so new to me. It definitely took more than one circle to really understand it.

I learned how to give others an opportunity to speak without me interrupting; I was able to learn more about them and ultimately just humanize them, and to realize we're having a human experience, that this is normal. I developed the ability to simply assert myself. I learned to assert what I needed, instead of being aggressive. My default was always aggression before. This was totally new to me.

And then, I think I started thinking differently because I started wondering. I got curious about what other people were going through. I knew my deep dark secrets. I knew the abuse and the things at home or in foster care that were happening. But I had this mind-set that I was the only one going through it. And in circle spaces, where everyone had an equal opportunity to share and to speak, I learned that other people were going through hard things, too.

I was discovering and developing empathy by hearing that everyone comes with a different story and different situations—that other people may have had a hard time or had things happening at home, too. I started to have more understanding of the people that I wanted to fight.

And I think that is what made me want to stay there and work on the issues I had. I was feeling validated about what I was going through—my experiences and the impact they had on me. I wasn't told that I was wrong for feeling that way. It was more of an acknowledgment that "Yes, this is what you're feeling, this is how you process this." And it gave me opportunities to think of new, different ways to hear other people's perspectives, how they were feeling and how they were processing their feelings.

For the first time ever, sitting in circle felt like a safe space. I felt safe. I learned the importance of using a talking piece to allow for true listening. I could be angry; I could be sad; I could be whatever I was going through. Circle created a safe space where we could come back in community and be vulnerable, and be transparent, and say what we needed. But say it in a way that didn't inflict harm or perpetuate harm.

Rosemary Anderson Prep School helped me get my GED at eighteen years old. I was at the YO Center for about three years. I was a ward of the court till I was twenty-one. Then the YO Center placed me in an internship as a front-desk receptionist. I worked as an administrative assistant at different places. Now I am working on my bachelor's degree in psychology and human development.

When I was thirty-five, some of the people who had worked at Rosemary Anderson Prep School when I was there encouraged me to apply for a position at Anderson. That included my mentor, Carl, who has stayed with me throughout my adult life. They felt like I had a powerful story and had a lot to share and could make an impact. I was hired to be the student engagement coordinator. And can you believe this? I have been the dean of students here for seven years.

Serving these kids is my purpose and my life's passion. I don't envision myself anywhere else.

The circle process is still being used in the school today. And some of the people who worked with me when I was a student still work here. The school still uses restorative justice. I didn't know how to name it then and I didn't know the history. I didn't know any of that. Now, I identify with students who have been hurt and who have hurt others. I remember how it was when I knew I was coming into what felt like a really uncomfortable place.

I work with students using circles. Sometimes I'll use a formal circle with the talking piece. But I'll also do it using another restorative practice called restorative dialogue. When using restorative dialogue, we aren't in circle, but the questions are the same. Whatever the format, the framework is still restorative justice. I also facilitate restorative justice circles and healing circles for the community outside of the school when something happens.

I also use restorative inquiries just trying to understand students and their trauma, to meet them where they are. I lead restorative circles when students get in trouble, with peer-to-peer conflict, and with teacher-to-peer conflict. I offer restorative dialogue, coming together in a structured space, discussing intent, impact, and what we need to reconcile our differences and stay in this shared space.

I like to share the history of restorative justice and how Afro-Indigenous cultures used restorative circles to have hard conversations. I help our students to realize their situation can be a learning experience, giving someone a chance to explain their intentions and for the victims to be able to explain the impact of harm on them. It's keeping close both those who have been harmed and those who have caused harm in community.

I still live in the same neighborhood that I did when I was born. I am working with students from the same exact streets and corners and intersections where I was selling drugs or stealing cars or fighting. I'm now working with the kids of the people who knew me as that person, and I'm sowing these good seeds. Restorative practices helped me and now I'm using it to help others. And so I'm also becoming restored as I am helping to restore others.

Part Three

Felony and Other Cases of Serious Harm

5.

Vehicular Deaths

Vehicular deaths present a conundrum: They are typically unintentional crimes, but the resulting harm is devastating. In non-DUI cases, the regular justice system is challenged by a discordance between the severity of the law broken—often something as mundane as an illegal turn or running of a red light—and the severity of the resulting harm.

From the perspective of a victim who has suffered a grievous bodily injury or lost a family member, the legal penalty for the driver who caused the accident can seem insignificant in comparison to the immensity of the victim's personal loss. And in some cases, the driver may not be criminally or civilly liable for the death or injury at all.

On the other side of a tragic accident, the driver responsible often feels deep remorse and a desire to express that to a victim's family. However, the regular justice system generally disallows direct communication between parties to a court case, which poses them as adversaries. In these cases, restorative justice can provide a parallel or alternative process for "accidental harm-doers" to express their remorse and concern for the family. For surviving family members, it provides an opportunity to have questions answered, to release anger, and obtain a measure of healing.

A Turn in the Road

Don Carney

I have been working in the field of restorative justice for over twenty years, as the founder and executive director of Youth Transforming Justice. Our mission is to disrupt the school-to-prison pipeline. One day while I was attending a professional conference, I got a phone call from a judge I knew who was also board president of the California Association of Youth Courts.

He asked if I could take fifteen minutes out of my day—right then and there—to explain to a district attorney how restorative justice works. I said yes, of course. The judge put the DA on speakerphone while I explained the philosophy and process of restorative justice.

Three months later, I found myself facilitating a case he referred to us, which would be the toughest and most rewarding restorative circle I had then facilitated in my career.

Brian was a seventeen-year-old young man who lived with his family on a horse ranch in Sierra County, in Northern California. This part of the state is well known for its rodeo shows. One February afternoon, he and his mother were driving to a horse show in an adjacent county. Brian was driving a big Suburban SUV hauling a four-horse trailer behind it; there were three horses on board. As they came to a large curve in the road, he hit a patch of black ice and temporarily lost control of the car. As he swerved, the trailer became unhitched and struck an oncoming truck head-on as it rounded the curve toward them. The impact killed the trucker, a man named Miguel, and the three horses.

In California, a driver must have a Class B license to haul a four-horse trailer (hauling a two-horse trailer requires only a regular driver's license). In violation of state law, Brian was driving without a Class B license. He was charged in juvenile court with vehicular manslaughter, a felony. A trial was held, and Brian was convicted. The district attorney had referred the case for restorative process in lieu of traditional probation conditions.

When I facilitate a restorative justice proceeding, I first have a conversation with all involved or impacted by the harmful incident to get their voluntary agreement to participate. After everyone agrees, I then have a private conversation with each individual to explore their feelings about what happened and what they need—or what they need to do—to make things right. I did all these pre-conference discussions by phone, since I resided in the Bay Area, some distance away from where this tragedy took place.

I then drove to the Sierra County probation office to hold in-person "precircles" with both families, before they met for the restorative justice circle. There were nine people from Miguel's family and four from Brian's; the large number of people impacted and the fact that we were dealing with a death made this an especially intensive restorative circle. It took just over nine hours.

The first precircle was with Brian, his parents, and his older brother and sister. I asked each one to share how they felt about what had happened. Lynda, Brian's mother, spoke first. She was obviously distraught but spoke with great resolve.

"This was a horrible accident. No one meant for this to happen." As Lynda began to cry, her husband put his arm around her shoulders, consoling her as she wept. Brian's brother was the next to speak. He focused on how responsible Brian had been growing up, and insisted the accident was not a reflection of Brian's character. The sister then chimed in protectively with comments about how mature Brian was and his ability to make good decisions, unlike most teenagers.

Brian, a good-looking young man with a pleasant smile, spoke last. He recounted the moment he felt the SUV skidding on the black ice and his struggle to regain control of the vehicle. At this point his entire body began to shake, and he struggled to speak. After a moment, he said: "I kept control of the car, but I lost the trailer." Brian buried his head in his hands. In a barely audible voice, he said, "It's horrible, just horrible; I killed a man."

My precircle with Miguel's family was next. Just as Miguel's wife Shannon began introducing herself and her children, she excused herself and abruptly ran outside. She vomited profusely and when she returned, apologized in embarrassment. I told her, "Listen, I cannot imagine how upsetting this is for you; don't apologize, we're going to deal with whatever happens." That set the emotional tone for the circle that followed that afternoon.

A senior probation official insisted that one of his officers be present in the room during the process. His request threw me for a moment; I worried that his presence would inhibit the conversation. I told him that I would need to get both families to agree before moving forward. The families reluctantly did so; many of them had driven hours to participate in the circle, and they wanted to go forward. The probation officer was a woman in her mid-thirties. She introduced herself by saying, "It is my job to ensure the safety of everyone involved in this process."

I sat on one side of the circle, and I asked the officer to sit opposite me on the other side of the circle. Brian and his family sat to my left and Miguel's family sat on my right.

Before the circle began, Shannon requested that we all start by watching the slide show from her husband's memorial service. Brian and his family agreed. The slide show chronicled Miguel's life as a successful immigrant from Mexico, his marriage to Shannon (a white, third-generation Californian), and the birth of their two children, Jerrod and Carmen. It also provided insight into

Miguel's dedication to his community; he volunteered at the juvenile hall, supporting immigrant youth by teaching them how to approach applying for a job. The slide show powerfully brought the essence of Miguel's meaningful life and kind spirit as a husband, father, and community member into the room. After twenty minutes, we were all in tears. Brian was clearly shaken to his core, processing his culpability in ending such a good man's life. It was the most powerful beginning to any restorative circle that I have experienced.

After a short break to compose ourselves, we resumed the circle. I asked Shannon to speak first. She told us how she heard about the crash and how she felt at the time. Her pain was gut wrenching to experience. Through a torrent of tears she said, "If it wasn't for my children, I would have ended my life."

Jerrod, the son, got the news of his father's death as he was about to give a business presentation at a Florida hotel. In a calm demeanor he credited to years of therapy, Jerrod described the surreal experience of hearing of his father's death behind the wheel while he was a continent away.

Carmen, Miguel's daughter, had just concluded her shift as an EMT and was driving home during a snowstorm. She got an alert from her dispatcher asking for her location and instructing her to stop where she was and wait for backup. When her fellow EMTs arrived, they delivered the wrenching news, collected her car, and drove her to her mother's home. Carmen was extremely agitated as she shared the pain of losing her beloved father; as she spoke, she repeatedly squeezed a tennis ball that she was holding in her right hand to manage her stress.

The extended family members followed next. Two aunts, an uncle, a cousin, a sister-in-law, and Shannon's mother all spoke about the pain of losing their beloved Miguel.

As you can imagine, there was a lot of anger expressed along

with the pain. It got so heated at one point that the probation officer got out of her seat and took a defensive stand behind her chair,
alarming everyone.

I reassured her it would be okay. I said, "This emotion is appropriate, and this anger is appropriate; nobody's going to get out of
control. Please return to your seat."

"But it's my duty to keep things safe," she responded.

"We're really glad you're here to help keep us safe, but right now
people need to express their feelings and that's okay." At that point,
she relaxed a bit and sat back down.

What is so enlightening about the restorative process is the
opportunity to understand an incident from multiple perspectives. People's assumptions are often challenged and changed in
the conversation. For example, Miguel's family members assumed
that Brian's family was affluent, since they owned a big ranch and
their insurance company immediately paid the maximum liability
award for Miguel's death. At one point during the session, Shannon said in an accusatory tone, "You rich people don't care about
people like us."

Brian's dad responded, "Yes, we were moderately well off, but
since this happened, I haven't been able to focus on my business,
and now I may lose it." That revelation showed how everyone was
impacted by a horrible mistake and tragic death.

I also have learned in restorative justice conferences that police
reports are not always complete or accurate. In this case, the police
report stated that Brian and his mother left the scene of the crime.
Marguerite, Miguel's sister-in-law, was married to a highway
patrol officer and was irate about that part of the report in particular. She wanted to know why they weren't being prosecuted for
leaving the scene of a crime in addition to Brian's charge of juvenile
vehicular manslaughter.

Lynda, Brian's mother, strongly refuted that accusation. "I did not leave the scene of the crime. I ran up the road around the curve to warn other drivers, fearing they might crash into the disabled truck." While Lynda went up the road, Brian went to check on the driver and horses. The scene was devastating—the driver and horses all dead from the impact. The crash occurred not far from a house on the road. A woman in that house heard the crash and came out to see what happened. She saw Brian, hysterical and hyperventilating, and said, "Come with me to my house and we'll call for an ambulance. It's too cold out to stay out here."

The conference clarified other mistaken perceptions as well. Shannon admonished Brian's family for not sitting with him in the courtroom during the trial, saying, "Any solid family would have supported their son by being next to him during such a difficult time." Lynda explained to Shannon that the court had ordered the family to sit apart from Brian during the proceedings.

After these exchanges, Shannon seemed deflated. She lamented, "I've been relying on this police report as a life preserver since my husband's death, and now that's gone too. I don't know what I'm going to hang onto now." Unlike what frequently transpires in a courtroom, no one from Miguel's family challenged the amended version of what happened that night. This is a testament to having people speak directly to each other rather than through attorneys.

After a break for lunch, we reconvened to hear from Brian and his family. Brian, his dad, brother, and sister all apologized for the death of Miguel. The family shared stories that were testimonials to Brian's kindness, empathy, and compassion. They concluded by asking Miguel's family for forgiveness.

Lynda spoke next. Without hesitation, she took responsibility for Miguel's death, acknowledging that she, who had a Class B license, should have been driving that night, rather than her son. She encouraged Miguel's family to blame her for the death, not Brian.

Shannon appeared relieved that Lynda took responsibility for her husband's death, but she was still full of anger: "Damn right, you are the adult and should have known better." Her daughter Carmen chimed in through tears, saying "You are absolutely correct, you are the one who is responsible for ending my dad's life." Her brother Jerrod, in a measured and composed tone, added, "I'm glad you are taking responsibility for my father's death; it was not your son's fault, it was yours."

At that point, Brian, full of remorse and anguish, blurted out, "I can't go on with my life; I've done something that can never be undone." He broke down sobbing. Lynda then shared with the group that her son had twice tried to kill himself since the crash. Just before the accident, Brian had been admitted to a college that offers courses in the rodeo business; he wanted to become a rodeo champion. Although this was his lifelong dream, Lynda explained that "he was so distraught and depressed that he declined the offer of admission."

It was at this moment that I could sense hearts beginning to shift in the room. In a voice full of surprising compassion, Shannon said, "Brian, there's been enough death; I don't want you to do that. If I can endure living, so can you," she said. "I most definitely want you to continue that pursuit; I want you to continue your life, I want you to thrive. This thing that has happened is horrible, but it shouldn't stop your life or your ability to move forward."

As part of the restorative plan, Shannon and her children requested that Brian's father continue Miguel's work in juvenile hall by providing marginalized youth with job training. Of Lynda, they asked that she share the story of Miguel's death at rodeo and horse show events, so that people in the horse business are clear

on the licensing required to haul a four-horse trailer. Both obligations were to run for five years, with no fewer than six juvenile hall
and rodeo/horse event visits per year. Shannon's request of Brian
was both straightforward and compassionate: She asked that he
seek therapy, never consider suicide again, and attend and graduate
from the rodeo college.

Brian and his mom and dad accepted the restorative plan as
requested. The probation officer had everyone sign off on the
restorative plan. Before concluding the circle, I expressed gratitude for everyone's participation, and for the deep expressions
of humanity I had witnessed. At that point, Shannon spontaneously asked Brian if she could give him a hug. After a moment of
silence and shock, he accepted her invitation and they embraced.
Tears flowed freely, as hugs were then exchanged by everyone in
the room.

The restorative plan that the two families devised was totally different than what would have resulted from the Probation Department's recommendation to the court. In the traditional process,
the victim's family would not have been involved in determining
the conditions of probation. Here, in the context of a restorative
justice circle, their input fundamentally shaped the accountability
plan for not only Brian but his parents as well.

Equally important, the conference resolved long-standing questions, mistaken perceptions, resentment, and anger that Miguel's
family held toward another family whom they had viewed as adversaries, sitting silently across from them on the other side of a courtroom. It gave a remorseful teenager the forgiveness he needed to
carry on with his life. This came about not through a formal trial
process, but because a grieving widow and the young man who
killed her husband were able to find each other's humanity, in conversation with one another.

The Necessity of Getting to Know You

Kris Miner

During and after my ten years of restorative justice work helping victims, survivors, former offenders, and teachers, I consulted and trained others across the United States. I believe the highest priority of restorative justice is to assist the healing of people who have been harmed. When putting victims first, I think it is important to remember that the severity of the law or rule broken does not always match the severity of the harm done.

This story is about a unique victim/offender dialogue regarding a traffic offense. In Wisconsin, turning left on a green light without yielding the right of way to oncoming traffic is considered to be a "failure to yield" traffic violation. It carries a $75 fine. This offender dialogue concerned a $75 ticket for what the law considered a minor offense, but it was much more to those involved.

Josh's parents had recently been through a divorce that was messy and difficult for him. On this occasion, the seventeen-year-old was heading home after having spent the weekend with his dad. Josh was preoccupied with that visit and the movie they had seen together. And, of course, he hadn't been a driver for very long. As he was driving through a residential area, he came to a traffic light at which he needed to turn left. Josh wasn't thinking about the rule that oncoming traffic has the right-of-way, even at a green light. As he turned left, he collided with a motorcycle carrying a man named Jack and his wife, Carol.

The impact caused Jack to fly through the air and smash into Josh's windshield and then slide off. Carol was also thrown, but in another direction, not onto Josh's car. She was trying to get over to her husband but couldn't because her ankle was broken, and the left side of her body was banged up. Josh was shocked but not seriously hurt when Jack slammed against his windshield. He got out of his car and went over to Carol to help her get to her husband before help arrived. Jack died shortly after getting to the hospital. He and Carol had a teenage son and a ten-year-old daughter.

Josh was ticketed, went to court, paid his $75 fine, and was given an order of court supervision.

Months later, Carol's kids started acting out in the wake of their father's death. Their teenage son, Jeff, started sneaking out and smoking marijuana. Then one day, after ten-year-old Shanna came home from school, Carol got a call from the school counselor. She said that Shanna had drawn a cartoon of herself hanging by a noose from a tree and said she just wanted to be with her dad. Carol knew she needed help and support for both her son and daughter. She remembered that, at the time of Josh's court appearance, something was mentioned about restorative justice, but no steps were taken to pursue it.

Dakota County traditionally referred traffic accident cases involving unimpaired drivers and their victims to restorative justice. (If impairment such as driving under the influence was involved, typically the offender would be prosecuted and sentenced to prison.)

Carol recalled how upset Josh was at the crash scene before law enforcement or others had arrived to help. She felt they had somehow made a connection, as he tried his best to move her. When she thought about that interaction with Josh, she thought restorative justice might be something that would help both her kids, who were struggling, and Josh, too. Even though it was about a year after the crash, she looked into it and found her way to me.

It is always important to begin a restorative process by getting to know both sides before bringing them together. First, I talked to Josh and his mom, Barbara. Because his parents had just divorced, and Barbara knew it had been quite difficult for Josh, she was protective of her son. She shared that he was going through a lot, too, and had his own feelings of worthlessness and remorse as well as survivor's guilt. I was also warned by his probation officer, to whom he reported for his court supervision, that sometimes Barbara would take over the conversation. So, when I explained to Barbara what would be happening with the dialogue, I made sure she understood that allowing Josh to speak for himself would be something that can help Josh, too.

Then I met with Carol alone at a restaurant. It was helpful to hear her struggles and her hopes for her children. About a week later, I met with Carol and her children, Jeff and Shanna. We had our prep session on a grassy area next to the parking lot of a Target store. I don't know why we met there, but it was what they wanted. If that is what they needed, it was fine. We were able to make it casual, and I think that helped them to feel comfortable with moving forward.

After meeting with everyone, I took some time to think about how best to handle the dialogue. I thought about how one mom might overtalk and be protective, while the other mom mostly wanted her kids to be able to talk. I decided to set the dialogue so that the moms would not sit at the table at first; instead, Josh would be peer-to-peer with Jeff and Shanna. Sometimes in these kinds of dialogues a child might get emotional, and we moms do what moms do—become mama bears and want to protect. But in this case, I felt it would be best if Barbara wasn't able to do that.

Typically, we use restorative justice questions such as: What were you thinking at the time? What have you thought about since? What do you think needs to happen to make things right? Sometimes with severe crime and violence, I'll use a storytelling format.

This time I used both the questions and storytelling. I had asked Jeff and Shanna ahead of time to think about who their dad was. I suggested, "Why don't you each select a story to tell about him?"

Shanna shared about the time she was afraid of needles and had to get an immunization for school. Her dad let her squeeze and squeeze his hand so hard that she left white imprints on his knuckles; she remembered that he took her for ice cream afterward. It meant so much to her that, even though she had been just a little girl when that happened, she still remembered and was able to tell this story about her dad. It was really sweet.

The stories that they shared about their dad to Josh were very moving to him. In fact, Josh even said, "I wish he would've been my dad." It was grief work.

Josh had a very strained relationship with his dad since his dad had left Josh's mother. Promises that had been made were not kept, and Josh was feeling right in the middle of it. Jeff's mother, Carol, had picked up on that at the court hearing, and I remember her saying to me the first time we met that hopefully he could learn about the healthy relationship she had had with her husband. She wanted Josh to know that not all marriages end up like his parents'. She had seen kindness in Josh by the way he tried to move her closer to her husband as they both experienced trauma together.

During the session with the children, the moms sat nearby and observed. And because they were there, they could really hear what their kids were saying for the first time. They got to observe the healing dialogue with the kids. Then we invited the moms to come to the table and add anything else they felt was needed. When the moms came to the table, they were just so deeply moved by their children's participation and the compassion received across the table that they really didn't have too much to add. There was some discussion, mostly mom-to-mom things.

When the time came for us to discuss what needed to happen to make things right, Carol and her children expressed that they felt that Josh had suffered enough. It was so healing that Carol, Jeff, and Shanna asked if they could hug Josh and his mom at the end.

When we were finished, I walked Josh and Barbara out the door. He absolutely looked like he was standing up straighter; the relief on his face was amazing. Later, when I followed up with them, they both agreed it was a great step in helping them to move forward.

When I went back inside to debrief with Carol and her children, they were all so pleased that they had crossed that bridge and met that challenge. I think back to the first time I met Carol, before I met her children. It was at a Buffalo Wild Wings restaurant. Those kinds of meetings are never just one hour long, especially with a survivor of a devastating crime or loss. You just make the time. We met over lunch, but the supper crowd was coming in before we were done. She needed all afternoon to talk.

Coincidentally, that very weekend Carol's family was having a one-year memorial event. They were going to take balloons and put a cross at the scene of the crash. She invited me to come. And she asked if I would please tell everybody that I was her cousin, because the extended family wouldn't like that she would have any-thing to do with Josh.

The fact that I went to that memorial and was part of walking with them, by their side, solidified our relationship even before the dialogue occurred. I was able to make suggestions like, "Why don't we try this? What do you guys think?" And they were able to help craft a dialogue process that helped all the parties recover from a traumatic event.

Once again, I had a front-row seat to healing.

6.

Murder and Other Serious Felonies

Restorative justice is often utilized strictly as an alternative to probation in low-level misdemeanors or cases in juvenile court. But restorative justice has a beneficial role to play in criminal cases involving adults as well—even in cases as serious as homicides. As the story in this chapter by Shaylie Pickrell and two of her clients illustrates, prosecutors are beginning to refer felony cases to restorative programs as an alternative to incarceration in midlevel felonies. Evaluations show that rates of reoffending are consistently lower among defendants who complete a program based on its principles of self-reflection, accountability, and repair. As the offender in this story explains, the restorative process required more effort and reflection than had multiple stints in prison, and for the first time in his life, elicited a genuine change in him.

When a murder is committed, there is obviously no way to restore a life taken or to repair fully the grief and pain of loved ones left behind. In cases of intentional homicide, restorative justice is not a substitute for a criminal prosecution, but it can play a powerful role as a supplement to a traditional justice system process. The stories shared here demonstrate how "victim-offender conferences," as they are known in this context, can provide answers and healing for surviving family members, as well as growth and a chance to express remorse on the part of perpetrators.

Such conferences generally take place months or years after a perpetrator has been convicted, when emotions have cooled and legal appeals have been concluded. Both parties must be open and ready: the victim's family to engage with the person responsible, and the perpetrator to give a full and open-hearted acknowledgment of responsibility. Victims and responsible parties must be carefully prepared in advance and the conference thoughtfully overseen by an experienced facilitator.

Restorative approaches to justice have traditionally not been used in cases of sexual harm, primarily because of concerns that survivors will experience secondary trauma. However, the potential benefits of restorative justice are many for survivors of sexual assault, whom the traditional justice system often fails spectacularly—either by failing to prosecute at all, or by shaming, blaming, and retraumatizing them in an adversarial proceeding. As a result, many victims of sexual assault do not even report the crimes against them. But survivors still often want to have the harm they experienced acknowledged and the perpetrator make amends. Many are also worried about perpetrators reoffending and want to reduce the risk that other women are harmed, which is not always an outcome of incarceration.[12] As the story in this chapter by Dr. Joy von Steiger illustrates, some survivors of sexual assault are finding healing by engaging in restorative dialogues with surrogate offenders who were not responsible for their violation, but who engaged in similar acts against others—a process known as "vicarious restorative justice."

Changing Normal

Shaylie Pickrell, Michael, and Sedric

My name is Shaylie Pickrell, and I am the director of operations and infrastructure for the Restorative Roots Project in Portland, Oregon. Our survivor-centered alternative to prisons program was created in 2021 to take felony cases, the first restorative justice program to do so in Oregon. The district attorney refers cases that are a fit for the program, which can include robbery, assault, and unlawful use of a weapon. As these are violent cases that typically involve a significant amount of trauma, we don't expect victims/harmed parties to be ready to talk in a month. We have an eighteen-month maximum time frame to prepare everyone fully prior to the conference.

The story that I share here is told from three perspectives: first from the harmed party, then the responsible party, and finally my own, as one of three facilitators who participated. The conference also involved translators, as two of the harmed parties spoke very little English. This was my very first case as a restorative justice facilitator, and I had no idea if my training would be sufficient. I had worked in suicide prevention, victims' advocacy, and youth corrections prior to taking this job. Those jobs had prepared me for a lot, but the journey that restorative justice requires was a different experience altogether, one that shattered my expectations.

This case also illustrates how restorative justice can "denormalize" violence and catalyze empathy and care for others in people who have caused harm.

Michael's Story

When I was seventeen, I worked at a Jack in the Box restaurant in Portland, Oregon, with two other employees. I was doing my regular thing, taking orders, handing people their food, when Sedric walked in the door. I thought he looked like a friendly guy—at least he seemed friendly at the start. And then, all of a sudden, he changed his tone, and he said that he was there to rob the store, and that he wanted all the money in the cash registers. At first, I thought he was joking because of my initial impression of him, but then I realized he wasn't. He started yelling at me and my two co-workers. Threatening us. We were all scared at that point. We didn't know what to do. I was the only one who spoke English well; my co-workers are from Mexico and speak Spanish as their first language.

He was looking at me and them, like, "Do they not understand?" And I said, "No, they don't speak English." He kept yelling at them in English. I had to translate for them. I was the one who got the money out of the cash registers and gave it to him. There weren't any other customers there at the time. He was implying that he had a firearm on him because he was reaching toward the back of his pants. He said he didn't want to hurt us, but that he would if he didn't get the money. He kept hollering at the woman who was our cook and the other guy who was working with me.

I think he got around $1,200 in cash, if I remember right. Then he ran out the door and sprinted away. And we all stood there in shock. It took us a little while to register what happened, and that we needed to call the authorities. The cook called them, and then she handed me the phone. I remember my voice was shaky. I was trying to explain to the officer what happened. It wasn't very long before the police came. They asked all kinds of questions about what happened, and we gave them the details. A couple of minutes later, they ended up catching someone who fit the description. They told us that if we wanted to go in their police car, we could make an identification to make sure it was the right person. They said he wouldn't be able to see us, but we would be able to see him.

So we did that and identified Sedric as the person who had robbed the restaurant.

After the police brought us back to the Jack in the Box, the manager was already there. She told us we could either finish our shift or go home. All of us were shaken up and wanted to go home. They closed the restaurant for the rest of the day. They gave us a case number and contact info and said that a district attorney was going to be in contact with us. I remember when I got home, my parents were asking me if I was okay. I just kept on telling them, "Yeah, I'm good." I stayed in my room that night, thinking of different outcomes that could have happened. I couldn't stop thinking.

All three of us met with the district attorney. She explained to us that we could go two ways with the case: a trial in court, or the Restorative Roots Project. They explained to us that the Restorative Roots Project was a way for us to express how crime had affected us and how we felt toward the man who did it, and that he would have to listen. Normally when people go to court, victims don't have a chance to explain how they were harmed, or to fully understand why the person did what they did. And through this program, we would be able to do all of that. We all decided to go forward with the Restorative Roots program.

After the robbery, I didn't really leave my house at all. I was a little scared of going out anywhere, because the authorities told us that Sedric had a warrant, and I thought that meant that he had a warrant out against us. We thought that he might have some kind of resentment toward us for identifying him and getting him arrested. We were scared that if he saw us going out for groceries or something, he might do something to harm us. When it came to leaving my house, I didn't want to go out alone. I don't remember all the details, but my parents told me that I kind of shut down. I know they were pretty worried about me.

It was about a month later when we met for the first time with three facilitators at the Restorative Roots Project: Shaylie, Brandon, and Stephen. In the first meeting, they asked us to write down what we felt at the time of the robbery, and what we were feeling since it happened. I know that really helped me a lot to process it. Another thing was just talking about the situation. At first, none of us really wanted to talk about it. So they didn't straight up ask us what had happened. Every meeting we had, they asked for a little part of the story, and if we felt comfortable to keep on going. They weren't trying to push us to give them all the details right then and there.

One of the first questions we asked was whether Sedric had any kind of resentment or beef with us and were we safe from him. At our second meeting the following week, the facilitators shared a little bit of what Sedric felt, including that he didn't really have any resentment toward us, which eased our minds and made things a little less stressful. That's when I started going out of the house more by myself.

Brandon, Stephen, and Shaylie were so helpful. We used both restorative justice–based activities (processing the experience, working on our support circle, preparing to talk with Sedric, finding out what community support can actually look like) and counseling to get ready for the big meeting with Sedric. The counseling was very helpful. We would go eat at a restaurant somewhere with Restorative Roots, or meet in the park, one of our homes, or wherever we felt most comfortable so that we could talk for a bit. They made us feel like we were in a safe place.

When we got closer to the time when we were going to meet with Sedric, they asked us if we were ready to have the conference. I told them I was ready to have the meeting. My two co-workers were a little more hesitant, but one ended up agreeing that he was ready, too. Our cook was the only one who wasn't as comfortable. She ended up writing a letter to Sedric, and her husband attended the meeting in her place. But when it came down to it, we all got to a place where we were ready to interact in some way.

We were all kind of nervous and scared because it had been a while—about sixteen months—since the robbery. We were all worried stuff might go the wrong way, or something might have happened that we didn't know about. We all had that in the back of our minds, and there was a lot of tension in that room. It was really awkward. We were sitting across from him in a circle; Sedric's brother was also there with him. Shaylie, Brandon, and Stephen told us that any time we felt uncomfortable, we could stand up and leave the room. Or if we needed to use the bathroom, or needed to take a break, we were more than welcome to do that.

You should know that before we had that big meeting, they had asked us if we wanted to speak first, or if we wanted Sedric to speak first. We all agreed we wanted to hear from him first. I could really tell that he was nervous. He said off the bat, "I'm sorry for what I did," and told us some of his background story: where he came from and what he was doing that day he robbed the Jack in the Box. He shared his story with us and what led him here, and his brother shared about their childhood and what Sedric was like growing up. His brother expressed what the effects of their upbringing were and what the impact of this new case was like on him personally: He said that he ended up moving out here to be with Sedric and to change his life as well. After they were done speaking, we took a break. When we came back into the room, I was the first one to speak.

I introduced myself. "I'm Michael; I was seventeen at the time of the crime and had been working at Jack in the Box for one year. If I have any sort of reaction like making jokes or laughing or smiling,

I'm not mocking you; it's just my way of coping with trauma and stress." You could tell he was listening to every detail. I told him my point of view and perspective of what happened that day.

"I thought you were a friendly guy, and that you were just messing around when you said this was a robbery. And then you raised your voice, and I realized you weren't joking."

I told him how scared I felt. "I was the only one who understood what you were saying, and I had to translate; I felt responsible for everyone in the situation." I told Sedric how worried and concerned my parents were and how it changed my view of going out and seeing people, how I shut down, and how the robbery affected my friendships and ability to prepare to graduate from high school. And he was actually surprised and shocked at some of the details because he hadn't noticed how scared we were that day. The seriousness of the situation set in as he leaned into our stories. It was interesting to me that he was shocked, in a way.

My co-workers' stories were a little different from mine. But they were also telling him about the way the crime had impacted them for a long time, and the shock of the situation. We were all just thinking the same thing: What could have happened if things had gone differently, if he'd had a gun and we didn't make it home that day? I remember we all shared that for the rest of the day; we didn't want to eat or do anything at all. We all shared the physical or mental struggles we had in getting back to "normal," or at least as close to what normal looked like.

When I got to thinking about our conference afterward, I realized that my first impression of Sedric that day I saw him at the restaurant wasn't wrong after all. He told us that since the incident, he had been going to therapy, attending church, and helping a lot in the community to try to be a better person.

That meeting really did help. We were able to come to good

terms. The plan we created said that Sedric would stay in therapy, stay in church, find a steady job, and keep working, so that he would not get to the point where he would be tempted to commit a crime again. We asked that he speak about his experience with people in similar situations to him or who have caused harm. The plan was set for six months of consistency for Sedric's church and therapy check-ins, and a timeline for speaking. It felt like a weight had been taken off my shoulders. I did feel a little relieved because he got to hear me out, and I got to hear him out. So, toward the end of the day of our meeting, I think we would both say that we had a good day.

The crazy thing is, right now I'm attending barbering school, and Sedric's brother attends there too! So, I've actually seen Sedric in person a couple times. And all those times we've met, there's been no hatred at all; it's been pure friendliness. There's no resentment toward each other. We even met to talk again about everything and catch up. I'm confident that he won't get into trouble again.

When I got home, though, my parents didn't take it completely the same way. I'm not sure how to explain it, but they were not as satisfied. They didn't get as much time with the Restorative Roots Project to process everything like we did, and they still held some resentment toward Sedric for harming their son. Being a parent in that situation and not knowing how I was feeling or what to do made them feel a sense of powerlessness, I think. But they said to me that if I felt good, that they were going to respect that. I am glad I went through it. We all had a chance to see stuff that we didn't see in ourselves before, like our inner strength and resilience. Each of us needed to work on things in our own personal growth, our past experiences, and how we processed and viewed things and what community could be like. It was a good experience with Shaylie, Stephen, and Brandon as our facilitators and support.

There is an important last detail that I want to share. That day of the robbery, I was actually not supposed to be working. A co-worker of mine had asked me if I could cover for them that day. You might think it wasn't my lucky day, but I feel like if I wasn't there, nobody would have been able to translate for the others and stayed, I guess, a little bit calm. In a way, I'm kind of glad I was there, but at the same time I'm not, due to the impact.

I would definitely say to anyone who is ever in this situation, who has been robbed or is impacted by crime and harm, that a restorative justice process is a much better way than going to trial. It was good to work with Restorative Roots and feel safe to meet with Sedric to hear about how he felt about what he had done.

Sedric's Story

My troubles started when I was in the second grade. The teacher would keep talking and it was awful. I typically have to keep doing something with my hands, but in second grade I just had to sit there. She would keep talking and I was just bored out of my mind. I think they put me in Special Ed because I was always in trouble, and they pretty much gave up on me in school.

When I was ten, me and my two brothers, we was playing inside a dumpster, with these matches, throwing them to each other. You know when you throw a match, it instantly goes out. But this one match, it didn't go out and it lit the whole garbage on fire. That's around the time when I started stealing more and getting into trouble. My mom was working two, three jobs, just trying to provide for the family.

When I was thirteen, I started smoking weed. I was already working a job at the age of thirteen. I used to go from place to place asking, "Hey, can I sweep the floor? Can I clean up? Can I do something to make a little money?" I used to go all around the city of Memphis and ask the people, "Can I work?" I was going in stores to clean but also stealing stuff out of stores. I went to juvenile prison for eight months when I was fourteen for aggravated assault. Was out for about three months then had to go back because I stole a car. I was in and out till I was eighteen. When I turned twenty-one, I eventually started robbing people in addition to stealing and went to prison from there. I was there for five years, seven months, and one week.

I wanted a new life, so I decided to move to Portland, Oregon. I got enough money and flew to Portland with $2,000 cash. I looked for work and lived where I could, mostly out of a car. I got enough money for a membership to a gym, where I could shower and sometimes sleep there. I was constantly working, working, working, getting fired, and also quitting sometimes. I had the mentality of, "If you're paying me minimum wage, and if I want to go out and smoke a blunt on my break, that's my time. You ain't paying me enough to ask me what I'm doing on my break. If you want to question me about my time, you need to pay me some more money." I might go into a job and say to myself, "Man, I don't like my manager. I might just quit for that." I was still adjusting, trying to let go of the prison mind-set and trying to adjust to how the world outside works, because in prison, you don't get fired from no job. So, I got fired a lot. Then I came up with this genius plan to go to Walmart and buy some disguises, then go to T-Mobile and Jack in the Box and rob them. I went to Jack in the Box first.

The police caught me. I thought I was going to prison for ten to fifteen years. When I got to the police station, I said I wanted to talk to a lawyer. That is how I met Tristen, my lawyer. She explained that there was this eighteen-month program where you talk to the victims of your crime. I thought it was a get-out-of-jail-free card, so I said yes. Then I met Brandon at Restorative Roots, and he asked me how I felt about things: "How are you right now? Maybe we can talk about the meeting. Maybe we can just talk about you. What's going on with you?" My response at first was, "I don't like telling people how I feel. Don't nobody care how I feel. I'm a man. Don't nobody care. Who cares about how I feel? I just got to get up and do it."

Brandon looked at me and he said, "Well, we care about how you feel. Talk to us about it." They even tried to help me get into an apartment, but I kept on refusing the apartment because I didn't want an apartment. I wanted to live in a car or live in a van. I feel like living in an apartment is boring. I know this is kind of crazy, but living out of a broke-down car is just kind of fun. My attitude about working was similar, just going from getting fired to quitting.

That's just some sickness that I had to get over with my mind; that's where Brandon and Shaylie came in. They let me know, "You don't need to think like this. It's not a healthy way of thinking." I think what helped me, when I was going through the job situation, is that they talked to me about what jobs I should think about. I wanted to be a truck driver. I wanted to try to get into the military, I wanted to try to do this, do this, do this. Then we got to talk about how to focus on one thing at a time, and then that's when I focused on truck driving. And once I focused on truck driving, it was like, "Okay, well then you can't have that mentality of, 'I'm going to do what I want to do. You ain't paying me enough. I'm going to do what I want to do.'" So they taught me the better way to think about stuff, and things are much better. I'm living out of my truck. I'm a truck driver, so I got a nice big comfortable bed. Got a little refrigerator and whatnot. I'm in my truck.

Then Brandon, Shaylie, and Stephen made me sit down and think about what I had done in robbing people and stuff. All the meetings with them helped me to think about the people I had harmed. But the one thing that really made me sit down and say, "Wow," was toward the end, when me and the harmed parties wrote letters to each other. They weren't ready yet for the conversation and felt more comfortable exchanging letters first to prepare. They wrote me a letter and I wrote them a letter.

One of the harmed parties wrote a letter that was very impactful on me. She said, "I have heard about people getting robbed, but I only thought that happened in movies." That blew my mind. Let me explain this: In Memphis, Tennessee, where I am from, I figured you get robbed, you get up and go about your business. You say to yourself, "Okay, I just got robbed today, but I'm gonna go back to work tomorrow." Before I say this, let me give you this little incident as an example. I remember one day I was getting my hair cut when the barber cutting my hair and another guy got in an argument. They ended up getting into a real fight. I got my back toward the fight, but I'm looking at them through the mirror. I'm like, "Man, can y'all hurry up and get finished fighting and get finished cutting my hair so I can go?"

In other words, violence was normal to me. But this lady was saying in her letter, "I couldn't sleep, I couldn't eat." She said she had to do therapy; she had to do all this stuff. And I'm like, "What?" She's saying this sounds like a movie, but what *she* said sounds to me like something that came out of the movie. For me, getting robbed and going back to work like everything's normal *is* normal. But this letter exchange with her got me thinking a little differently. In the letters, they wrote me about what they went through after the robbery, how it impacted them and their families and ability to live their lives. They also asked me questions they had, like why I did what I did and what was my childhood like. I answered all their questions and told them about myself and what got me here.

Now this new thing happened a couple months ago. My little brother, he moved up to Portland and he worked at Burger King. He called me one night and said, "Bro, we just got robbed tonight. Somebody came through the drive-through window and robbed me." We was laughing about it like it was nothing.

A while later he called me and said, "Bro, they telling me to come to court because of this robbery." I'm saying, "Oh man, you gonna go to court and testify on this man? Man, you old snitch! You a real piece of work. You need to get yourself together." But then I hung up the phone from talking to him, and I thought, *What the f**k is wrong with me? I can't believe I did that.* I didn't even ask him, Was he okay? Did he need to talk about it? How was he feeling?

I called him back and I said, "Hey little bro, how are you really feeling? Because I know I've been giving you a hard time." He said, "Man, I'm good. You know I'm good." But then I had to tell him, "Bro, I just want to apologize to you because at that moment I wasn't thinking about your feelings. I wasn't thinking about how you might actually feel—like, were you afraid to go back to work? I wasn't thinking about that."

He said he wasn't. But still, I called Brandon to talk about it. He was like, "Sedric, you're showing growth by the fact that you're thinking about the impact on other people. Maybe this time it didn't register as fast as you want it to. The next time when something happens, it'll register, like, 'Let me not clown around with you right now. Let me see how you're feeling.'" So this was one of the changes in me from being a part of Restorative Roots. I'm thinking about other people, how they be feeling and the consequences of what I do when I go out there. How is that going to make this person feel?

But they told me there was still more things to do before I met with the people I harmed. It was still a lot of more prep that needed to be done. So it was just still back and forth going to meetings. And then I started truck driving. And one thing they told me is, "We'll never stop you from going to work for a meeting. We'll reschedule the meeting around your work." But I was over-the-road truck driving, so we had to start doing virtual meetings. They were always very flexible. They was so flexible, goodness gracious—late to meetings and all type of stuff, I was that person.

They was talking to the harmed party, too, and they just kept talking to me and getting us built up for a meeting between us. It was two or three months later after we had written those letters to each other that they said, "It's come time for the actual sit-down." I remember the night before the meeting, Stephen came to me and he said, "Hey man, you ready?" I looked at him and I said, "Yeah, I'm ready. What you mean?" He was like, "This is going to be emotional for you."

I'm like, "Nah, Stephen, it ain't going to be that." Then he said, "It's going to get emotional." I said, "Man, I'm going to be good then."

The day of the meeting, man, I thought I was ready. But I tell you, when I went into the room, I lost track of everything I wanted to say. I was just so confused. The emotion kept coming up. I'm crying. I'm like, "What am I crying for?" It really hit me. All three of them and their families were talking about how I impacted their life.

One of the harmed parties was saying "I'm just afraid to go out and hang with my family, to go to my son's soccer game, because of what you did. I don't feel comfortable going outside." The other harmed party's husband said how I put a big strain on her life. She had to go to doctors because she didn't want to eat; she had to go to therapy. Michael, he just really kind of laughed it off. That's one of the things about me and Michael, we just laugh everything off. But his parents were more concerned about him. Once you hear about all those things, you do think, *Wow—I did all this to these people.*

I went to prison in Tennessee for the same things I did here in Oregon. But the thing about it is, in prison, you don't know how the harmed party feels. You just go to court and get some time and go to prison. Once you in prison, you don't hear nothing from them, they don't hear nothing from you. I didn't know how what I did affected them. I don't even know what the people I harmed in Tennessee even look like. I went to prison, did my little time, and came back home, and that's it.

But with this, there was just so much emotion. I was thinking at one point, *Man, you know what? I wish I would've just went back to prison instead of having to deal with their emotion and feelings.* Seriously, I had to sit there and listen to it when they got angry, when they were literally telling me how I made them feel, giving me that raw emotion, telling me all that. I was like, "Man, I wish I would just have went on to court and did that ten to fifteen years."

Then it was time to come up with what they called my "restorative plan." And it was different than I expected. One harmed party was very heavy into the church and stuff, so he wanted me to be part of the church life. He asked me to go to church on a regular basis. I already go to church, so that was a wonderful thing. The other harmed party wanted me to go to therapy, which I was already doing. So I just had to continue on with my therapy stuff. They all wanted me to get a stable job, which I have now. They wanted me to speak about my experience to a group of individuals. I volunteer at church and speak to the youth that I work with in the church services, and I spoke at Restorative Roots Project's first fund-raiser with Michael to share our story. And I decided on my own accord that I wanted to set up a payment plan to help one of the harmed parties with her medical bills, because of the stress that I caused her. I hope that her therapy helped her feel more safe, because I know she chose not to come to the meeting. Her husband came in place of her. I don't know if she feels safe again. I would hope that she's feeling safe to this moment, but I don't know.

I believe that God wants the best for us. I hate to say it like this, but I really look at it as a blessing in disguise. I feel like this has become a true blessing for me because I did need the help of Brandon, Stephen, and Shaylie to get readjusted back into society. I needed the help so I can start thinking about others' feelings and how my actions impact other people.

I do feel like the restorative justice process was something that I really needed and benefited from; I just hate that it had to come about the way that it did. I am so happy that I was able to be a part of this program and put my story here.

Shaylie's Story

A restorative justice process is more than having a conversation and forgetting it ever happened; it's about fostering real growth and healing on all sides. That process takes time. It might seem as if eighteen months is a long lead-up to a restorative justice session, but there are many needs to meet on all sides. For victims, we need to provide them with a say in the process, allow them access to resources that may be hard to obtain on their own, and provide space to share the impact of the harm or crime. We need to provide them with the opportunity to ask, "Why?"—to let them heal.

For offenders/responsible parties, we need to provide the time to reflect and to take accountability in a meaningful way. We give them access to resources and therapy to understand their reasons for committing the crime, because often harms and crimes are done out of an unfulfilled need. All of this is important before putting them face-to-face with the human beings they have hurt. We focus on needs and community building first. If someone doesn't have their basic needs met and doesn't trust us, there is no way they will be able to be open and honest and be able to process it all. We also understand that many cases involve mutual harm, and it takes time to unravel and discuss these complexities.

This was a complex circle to facilitate. We had three harmed parties and varying levels of language barriers to navigate. Our circle included a total of fourteen people: the responsible party and his support person, two harmed parties, one surrogate (the husband of one of the harmed parties), four of their support people, two translators, and three facilitators. Hearing the impacts of the harm on all sides, sharing who they were before and after the harm occurred, pausing to take a break when emotions became elevated, and creating a plan for restoration took a total of eight hours. We ate together and created a plan for restoration together.

At the end of our session, the room was both heavy and soft. So much emotion had been shared, including laughter. Sedric told us he had about a fifth-grade reading level and doubted his ability to express himself. But he feels so deeply and is very smart; he was just never given the opportunity to show it. To be able to help lift him up to realize his potential has been an honor.

The harmed parties amazed me with their level of resilience and ability to forgive. I saw that this is possible when people are allowed to be a part of a process of dialogue and resolution, rather than watching as a spectator through a glass partition or a bench in a courtroom. Although they were impacted to different degrees and participated in different ways, the growth and love they displayed is what keeps me doing this work. One opted to write a letter and have her husband participate in the circle in her stead. One of them just wanted Sedric to be okay and grow and learn from this. And Michael, who had just graduated from high school, showed how mature and resilient our youth can be when given the platform to say what they think and what they need.

The degree of insight and impact that emerged from these amazing individuals—Sedric, Michael, and his two co-workers—was something I had never seen before in all of my years of counseling victims and offenders. We worked hard over a period of eighteen months to develop trust and provide a safe space for everyone involved, and by the end the harmed parties considered us family. We helped them to buy school supplies and sign their kids up for soccer; they invited us over for dinner, called when times were hard and when there was news to celebrate. Watching Sedric's growth and the harmed parties' healing and willingness to forgive was one of the most beautiful parts of this process—furthering the roots of care, connection, and community. The individuals involved had been through so much in their lives, but they all showed what resilience and community support can do. Michael, having to experience an essential part of life and growing up while experiencing this; Sedric, understanding the impact of his decisions; the harmed parties, processing trauma and trusting complete strangers to help guide them—this is what makes them all amazing.

Although the case is finished, the harmed party who did not attend the restorative conference is now wanting to write Sedric another letter. Every person reacts and processes trauma and stress differently. For her, the robbery and trauma that resulted led to a hospitalization, surgery, therapy, and the need to take large portions of time off from work. The third harmed party, who also received therapy after the robbery, continues to ask how Sedric is doing and wishes him well in his continued growth. One of them even shared that, "In the twenty years I've been in this country, this is the first time I ever felt like I belong." I think it's because the process gave them support, access to therapy, and a sense of community that they otherwise wouldn't have had—certainly not if they had gone through the traditional criminal justice process.

As restorative justice facilitators, we often hear "thank you" from participants, but I can't help thinking that all we did was foster the strength that they have carried with them their whole lives. They did the hard work; all we did was provide the space for their voices to be heard in full. No matter how many cases we receive, how many circles we facilitate or community members we meet, I will never feel like "the expert," as all we are doing is fostering a place for community and centuries worth of these practices to grow and shine through.

Even the Cops Were Crying

Steve Wilson

I met Bob for the first time in a contact visiting room at our local jail. He was just a few years younger than me, in his late thirties, a handsome, dark-haired man who rarely smiled. He had little reason to smile at the time. He was charged with murder, and Oregon had the death penalty.

The murder had happened almost twenty years earlier—the shooting of a woman named Diane on New Year's Eve. At the time of the homicide, Bob was nineteen, a white member of a mostly Black gang who had been brought up in a steady middle-class household. Since the homicide, Bob had dropped out of the gang. He started working. He went to church. He got married. Bob and his wife had two little girls.

While he was getting his life back on track, the victim's aunt, a woman named Theresa, continued to put pressure on the Cold Case Squad to solve Diane's murder. Theresa was the angriest member of Diane's family and the most vocal. She was also persistent. And after nearly two decades, the police finally made an arrest.

Which is why I was in jail introducing myself to Bob as his defense investigator. My job: locate witnesses, perform interviews, and generally test the facts of the state's case.

Usually, when I first meet a person accused of murder, they deny, deny, and deny. There's no inherent trust between a defendant and his legal team, and I have been sent off on many wild goose chases to try and prove a defendant's alibi. When I first started working as a defense investigator, I usually believed whatever my clients told me. Later, I learned to listen but to believe only what I could confirm. Nobody wants to be locked up, and people go to great lengths to avoid it. But I also learned that guilt spawns not just denial to others, but denial to oneself. Over time, I've come to see that a large part of the fiction that defendants tell me emerges from a fear of facing their own actions, a fear of feeling responsible for taking another person's life.

For Bob, those two decades came with sleepless nights and a heavy load of guilt. He once told me that he regularly had night-mares in which somebody was chasing and trying to kill him. He would wake up screaming. When he and his wife first started shar-ing a bed, Bob's nightmares frightened her. Bob knew why he was having nightmares, but he could never share the reason with her.

So, when an old gang-friend of Bob's caught a charge and decided to trade his knowledge of what Bob had done for a better plea deal, in some ways it was a relief. Right from the beginning, Bob admit-ted his guilt and accepted that prison was in his future.

Bob's candor with his legal team, his remorse, and his accep-tance that he was going to and needed to pay a price for his earlier actions, was the first of three remarkable moments in Bob's case. Right from the beginning, Bob's case was different.

In homicide cases, and especially in capital cases, I am usually very busy tracking down witnesses, requesting documents, explor-ing the background of the prosecution's witnesses, etc. There was some of that in Bob's case, but the mitigation specialist was bus-ier than I was. Mitigation specialists are investigators, primarily working on homicides, who gather information about the defen-dant's life, achievements, and limitations in order to tell the defen-dant's story and to place the actions into context. We requested Bob's school records, interviewed friends and family, reviewed the discovery, and built a timeline. In addition, Bob's attorneys, work-ing through a defense-initiated victim's outreach (DIVO) advo-cate, began a dialogue with Diane's family. DIVO advocates, often trained as social workers, are rarely-used intermediaries between a defense team and a victim's family.

That was the second remarkable event in Bob's case.

Family members of a homicide victim are often but not always part of plea negotiations. They can be, and often are, out for revenge—Old Testament eye-for-an-eye type stuff. The family is not the ultimate decision maker; that falls to the district attorney as a representative of the state. The family plays a large role, however, and can speed up or slow down a case if they demand a certain type of sentence.

In Diane's case, the family was large, close-knit, and humbly Christian. I say humbly Christian because the family wasn't self-righteous or vindictive. They didn't want an eye for an eye. Their perspective was more holistic, seeing the value in forgiveness and the consequences of clinging to anger and hatred. They were looking at a bigger picture.

That doesn't mean they were willing to walk away and forget about Diane's murder. Without constant pressure from the family, the Cold Case Squad might never have reopened the case. The family wanted justice. But their justice was based on a need for understanding and closure rather than revenge.

Many months before Bob's eventual sentencing, our victim's outreach advocate connected Diane's mom, Sarah, with Bob's wife, Eileen, first by phone and then in person. Sarah was wise enough to understand that Bob's actions would have a long and profound effect on his wife and children, and she was able to separate her feelings about Bob from the people around him. She knew that Bob would face punishment, but she also knew that punishment didn't need to include the people close to him who bore no responsibility for his actions.

Through their conversations, Diane's family and Bob's family found common cause. Both were in pain because of what Bob had done. There was no getting around that. Time couldn't be rolled back. The justice system was not going to allow Bob to walk away just because he had found God and raised a family. But both families could connect and agree that, as much as possible, the people around Bob—all of those rocked by the ripples of his actions—should be spared the penalty that Bob must accept and should try to help each other get through the coming experience with love and dignity.

The meetings between Sarah and Eileen affected me deeply. Once again, I had never worked on a case where the sides had made an effort to get beyond adversarial confrontation. Those two families showed immense bravery when they chose to meet each other and to be honest about what had happened and what the future held. They prayed together. I'm an atheist and it would be hypocritical for me to say that I think they were talking to God, but I believe they were reaching for compassion under very difficult circumstances and were expressing hope and commitment together in a way that had deep meaning and built trust.

Finally, after a lot of discussion, Diane's family agreed that the death penalty should be off the table. About a year after his arrest, Bob pled guilty to murder and was sentenced to serve twenty-five years in a state penitentiary. On the record, the judge accepted the plea, read out the sentence and all the mandatory small print that comes along with the conclusion of a criminal case, and Bob's case ended for the public at large. The court reporter went home.

Then, the third remarkable event happened. Bob, the victim's family, the judge, the prosecutors, the cops, and the defense team all entered a large jury room. There were a couple of long conference tables, chairs surrounding them and scattered about. Off to one side was another, smaller table with two chairs that faced each other.

Bob was placed at the small table, his back to a wall, facing everybody else in the room. He was wearing a pink jail coverall. I don't think he was handcuffed but his ankles might have been. A couple of deputies stood nearby. It could have been a scene in an interrogation room. But instead of a police detective taking the chair across from Bob, it was going to be somebody from Diane's family.

One of the deputies explained how the process would work. Any member of Diane's family could speak to Bob, ask him questions, tell him what they were thinking. They could speak from their seats, or, if they wanted to, they could sit in that second chair and face Bob. Then the deputy invited Diane's family members to come forward.

Diane's mother, Sarah, was the first to move. She climbed out of her chair, walked across the room, and sat down opposite Bob. The two looked at each other, separated by three feet of plywood and laminate. Sarah said, "I want to know what happened."

So Bob told her. It took some time. Bob went back to his childhood, describing who he was and how he was raised, his poor relationship with his father, his upbringing in a middle-class family, not lacking for material things, but not a family full of love. He didn't just describe the incident but gave the background and context. Bob struggled at times. He had trouble explaining the apparent discrepancy between his safe upbringing and his gang life. It vaguely centered around his lack of connection to his parents, which built in him an anger that had no point of concentration. Bob's anger was directed at everybody.

Eventually, Bob got to the moment that ended Diane's life and changed his.

It was New Year's Eve when Bob and a friend stopped at a

convenience store during a drive across town. Bob had been drinking, and in his pocket he had a small .22 pistol that held two bullets. Bob wasn't familiar with pistols. At the time, gangs still settled their differences with fists and knives.

Bob had found the pistol in the glove box of a car when he and his buddies were out jockey-boxing—looking for unlocked cars and taking anything of value from them. The gun was silver, a few inches long, and the entire thing fit in the palm of Bob's hand. When he first dragged it out of the glove box, he thought it was a novelty lighter, and, sticking a cigarette into his mouth, Bob held the pistol up to the end of the cigarette and pulled the trigger. Luckily, that bullet didn't hit anybody. Later, in his bedroom, Bob shot himself in the hand trying to reload the gun.

So, armed, drunk, and pissed off at the world, Bob entered the convenience store and got in line behind an attractive woman about ten years older than him, and they began to flirt. Bob was a good-looking guy, confident and chatty, and the two continued to talk as they left the store. Bob walked the woman to her car, and suggested she follow him. They drove to a quiet spot a couple of blocks away and parked.

When Bob approached Diane's car, she was angry and ready to tell him about it. As Bob stood outside of her car she began cursing and insulting him for dragging her to this spot and who the f**k did he think he was?

I remember, at this point in the story, a smattering of laughter from Diane's family. One of them said, "That sounds just like her!"

I was astonished. These people were listening to a description of how their loved one had died, from the mouth of the man who had killed her, and they were laughing. They were experiencing the moment with Bob. They were inside the story.

Bob tried to explain what he still didn't really have words for. Diane's response triggered all the rage and frustration and unresolved pain in his life that was lurking just outside of his conscious world. He pulled the tiny pistol from his pocket, put it against Diane's head, and fired.

It was a small pistol and made a small sound. He felt an instant rush of regret and misery. Bob and his friend fled.

Bob was openly weeping by this point and the rest of the room was silent and still. There were about thirty people watching him. Bob's voice came in bursts and cracked. I don't think anybody doubted his honesty. He hadn't tried to make himself look good. Sarah was still sitting in the chair across from Bob. She was crying. Did she reach a hand across to comfort him? I don't know—my memory of the moment is nearly all about the emotions—but if she didn't reach across, there was a feeling of that kind of connection between the two.

I remember feeling my own tears and looking around the room. Most of the victim's family were crying. More surprisingly, almost everybody else was too: the judge, the prosecutors, the sheriff's deputies, the defense attorneys—nearly all were wiping their faces. Even the cops were crying.

Not everybody in the room felt the same way, however. Aunt Theresa, the person who had pressured the police to solve Diane's murder, stood up, shouting: If Bob was such a good guy, if he felt so much remorse, why hadn't he turned himself in? He had let her family suffer while he got on with his life.

Theresa had made a statement in court after Bob apologized during the public proceedings. Hands stuffed in her pockets, she called him out for being a hypocrite who was only contrite after being caught, describing her own flooding anger and the need to keep her hands contained so that she wouldn't attack him. In the private jury room, Theresa screamed something akin to "Rot in hell"—and stormed out of the room.

Yet most of the family seemed to be moved by Bob's narrative. I can only speculate that his story might have provided them with the first real sense of closure in two decades. When I say closure, I don't mean that they felt at peace or that Diane's death no longer weighed on them, or that they no longer felt a deep loss. But grief they experienced over Diane's death must have been compounded by important questions that had never been answered: Who did this? Why?

One detective later said in a newspaper article that the experience in the jury room was a singular moment in his career. Did he and other officers too feel the sense of a circle completed? Or were their tears a response to the emotion pervading the room? As a longtime member of the defense, I have a hard time believing that police officers feel empathy for defendants, but that might be unfair.

My own feelings were complex. Some of my tears fell just because of the sensation inside the room. Community is built on shared emotional experiences, and the emotion in the room was strong and pervasive. I got caught up in the emotion expressed by Bob and by Diane's family. I also felt empathy for the family finally getting the knowledge they had long sought about what happened that night. How many difficult nights had they struggled through? How many missed birthday celebrations, comments from friends, and sudden inexplicable waves of sadness had penetrated their defenses?

I had empathy for Bob, too. He had done something horrible. But carrying such a secret must have been exhausting. He was finally able to lay part of that burden down. When I talked to Bob years after the case concluded, he told me that this was true. The nightmares that had plagued him before his arrest had continued when he was in jail waiting for a trial. But after his meeting with Diane's family, the nightmares stopped.

And finally, one part of my own emotional response was seeing—feeling—a healthy conclusion to a case. I have been involved in over 1,000 criminal cases since I began working as a defense investigator in 2003. For the most part these cases have been bureaucratic and unemotional—the criminal justice machine churning along, taking in broken people on one end and spitting out broken lives on the other. The federal government even has a grid to help with sentencing: Take one's criminal history on this row and the seriousness of the crime in that column and match the two up to determine the sentence. It is inherently impersonal and unresponsive to the specifics of the case and the individual. Bringing humanity to the case, seeing the humanity in the people involved, is the mark of a rare and good attorney, whether for the defense or the prosecution.

So, being involved in this somewhat deadening process, especially when you work for the defense and a good day is getting life in prison for your defendant rather than a death sentence, it is easy to get burned out. It's easy to feel that there is no point. That the system is broken. That every time a person is incarcerated, allegedly to rehabilitate the person, what in fact is happening is that the person is being ostracized and warehoused for a while. And in the meantime, their spouses, partners, and children pay a price that is unacknowledged and ignored, a price that often ends up being expressed through drug and alcohol abuse and generational violence. Crime victims and their family members pay that same price, if not more.

Sometimes I think of a criminal incident as a moment when pain is transferred. In my mind somebody like Bob was carrying a backpack full of pain, and when he shot Diane, he took some of the pain from his backpack and put it into the backpacks of his wife, his kids, and Diane's family. But when an act of violence takes place, all that new and extra pain can be too much to carry. Yet our justice system does not adequately address the need for healing. We act as if the crime is over because the bad guy is behind bars. But what we are really doing is pretending the pain doesn't exist.

When Bob met with Diane's family in that jury room and recounted his story and that of Diane's last moments, some of that pain was released. I had never seen that happen before. In that moment I saw that there is another way.

There were some unique circumstances about Bob's case that facilitated a restorative victim-offender dialogue. Both families were people of faith. Bob genuinely wanted to make what amends he could, little as they were. Diane's family truly wanted not to carry hatred with them. Both sides were willing to be vulnerable and proceed with a common purpose.

Also, a lot of time had passed. Most murders are solved quickly and at the time a plea is reached, or trial is underway, the victim's family is still mourning and often in a place of anger, and the defendant may be clinging to denial or bombast. So much time had gone by in Bob's case that many members of Diane's family had already come to terms with her death—some kind of internal understanding, some kind of peace within themselves, however incomplete.

Diane's family and Bob and his family came into that room with open hearts, showing a bravery and compassion that was inspiring. Sarah could have straddled the chair and let forth with righteous anger, as her sister did. But she didn't. She just wanted to know how her baby died. She wanted to hear the end of the story.

And Bob could have protected himself. Faced with a large group, expected to speak deeply and honestly in an institutional setting

surrounded by strangers, Bob could have told a story that minimized his role, defended his actions, or made excuses. He could
have simply said he was high and he didn't remember. But he didn't.
He explained what had brought him to that place, both physically
and emotionally. He took responsibility for the death and showed
his own pain and regret without asking for pity.

In addition to the unique way that both Bob's and Diane's
families handled themselves, the entire criminal justice machine
that processed Bob's case—from detectives to prosecutors to the
defense attorneys and the judge—was also willing to do things differently. One of the detectives told a reporter afterward that in
twenty-five years on the force he had never experienced anything
like it. There was a willingness everywhere you looked for this case
to proceed under its own, unique terms.

Bob's participation in the restorative justice process wasn't an
escape from a serious sentence of incarceration. But the fact that
the offender-victim dialogue was allowed to proceed in tandem
with the judicial process meant that the judicial system offered
some healing and closure instead of just punishment.

The events that happened in that jury room ten years ago still
move me. It is one of the few times in my career when I have felt
that the justice system really worked. And it worked because it
allowed for the humanity of everybody involved to be expressed.

The way our criminal justice system is constructed makes an
outcome like the one I witnessed difficult to organize. We start
with two adversarial parties struggling to limit the amount and
type of information the other party gets to share at trial. There can
be a lot of resistance and resentment between the two sides. Sometimes the enmity between the opposing attorneys can become very
personal. The system is designed this way. It is designed to have
individuals competing against each other, trying to outdo each

other in their mastery of the law and judicial procedure, and somehow justice is supposed to emerge.

The cost of this system is true understanding. Like spouses in a loveless marriage, the parties can be civil, respectful even, but their hearts are closed to each other. They assume that because they are on opposite sides of a legal issue, they must be on opposites sides of all matters related to the case.

And when a person is convicted and sentenced, the tone almost inevitably changes to one of punishment and rancor. Victims' families are often given an opportunity to speak and generally use it to express anger and resentment. While sometimes defendants may apologize and weep and take responsibility, most of the time they sit silently. Often this is on the advice of their attorneys, who are hoping to protect some appellate issue.

Even in Bob's case, the defense attorneys were reluctant to propose a meeting with Diane's family. Such a move went against everything that they had been trained for and all they had learned in their legal practice. Bob had to insist that the meeting take place.

When a trial is all over, the defendant is usually sent to prison never to have contact with the victim's family again, leaving all that pain to be carried around by all those people, with the rest of us acting as if the pain no longer exists. I had hoped, after Bob's sentence, that things might change. I have no doubt that everybody in that room was moved by what they experienced. They all saw how the system could work. Unfortunately, our criminal justice system is profoundly ill-equipped to recognize individuality. It is not designed to bridge gaps between the prosecution and the defense.

Rather than institutional changes, what I have seen is a gradual growth in awareness that there are more people to be concerned about than just the victims or their immediate families. I have seen judges openly recognize that there is value in listening, and I have been party to conversations and even trials in which the prosecution seemed to understand that there was more to an individual than the criminal charge they were currently fighting.

So, we are not there yet. But even after all these years, I can still feel hope when I think back to that moment when a killer and a victim's family laughed and cried together.

Honesty from the Heart

Rose Gordon

My story involves a case I received as the restorative justice facilitator for juvenile cases in Taos, New Mexico. Greg had shot and killed his friend Mark when they were both fifteen. They had recently become the youngest members of a local gang. Greg was sentenced to three years at the Taos Youth Detention Center until he turned eighteen. The charge against him was "Child Abuse Resulting in Death."

The victim's father, Alan, had separated from the boy's mother when Mark was around twelve. Alan frequently traveled to job sites around the country as a building contractor and was a thousand miles away at the time of the murder. He had continued to travel for work and was heard to say that he never wanted to see the house where his son had died again. At his request, the court included a provision for him, as the father of the victim, to meet Greg—if Greg were willing and his caseworker at the detention center believed Greg was up to it.

Within a year of Greg's release date, Alan called the superintendent of the facility to ask if a restorative justice circle could be arranged there. Attending with me and my co-leader would be the superintendent, Greg, Greg's caseworker, and Alan.

At seventeen, Greg came to my restorative justice office from the Taos Youth Detention Center. He was accompanied by a guard who stayed in the reception room as Greg followed me to my office. Greg was wearing the bright blue shirt and gray pants that was the uniform at the center at the time. He had dark hair and dark eyes, and he greeted me with a quick smile and a hesitant "Hello, Miss" as he sat across from me.

I always have a preconference meeting with everyone involved before we hold the actual circle. These meetings, always in person for the offender, but occasionally by phone for the victims, give everyone an opportunity to learn more about my process as a facilitator. They're a vital chance for me to meet the people involved and to establish a plan for the circle.

I had spoken with Greg's caseworker on the phone, who stated that Greg had matured during his time at the center and was ready to meet with Alan. In a separate phone conversation with the superintendent, I learned that Greg had agreed to participate in the restorative justice circle in part because he wanted to talk about how it "really went down."

I then contacted Alan by phone and explained the restorative justice process and asked about his reasons for requesting the circle. For his part, he wanted to hear directly from Greg, in an atmosphere that was private and separate from the legal system, about what had happened on the day of his son's killing.

The center agreed to drive Greg the 120 miles from the facility to my Taos office for an in-person meeting with me.

I was uncharacteristically nervous. I had already read Greg's file, which noted that there were four other men in his family who were in prison or institutionalized for murder. They had all killed someone, and now so had he. I placed my chair a few feet from where Greg sat, and we began to talk about his immediate family and his time at the Youth Detention Center.

My basic preconference questions include "Is there anyone who would notice if you were having a hard day, even without you saying a word about it?" (to establish presence or absence of support—a risk/resiliency question). And "What are your hopes or dreams for the future?" (hopes and dreams support resiliency). I had designed the meeting intake forms by modifying some of the language in the Youth Risk and Resiliency Surveys that are voluntarily used

every two years by high schools in the United States. This is to
have a better understanding of both the youth's emotional development and support system as well as risk factors. As I held Greg's file
on my lap, I realized that he was nervous. As we talked, his right leg
tapped the floor continuously.

I asked Greg about the day of the shooting. He took a deep
breath before recounting how he accidentally shot his best friend
while trying to impress a girl with a gun. What he really seemed
to want me to understand is that he didn't run away from the scene
immediately the way the police stated. "I didn't," he said. "I don't
remember calling a gang member, but I guess I did, and then my
lieutenant, who I reported to in the gang, told me to just run, to
get out of there. The police got it wrong! I didn't just run and leave
him there to die. It wasn't like that."

"I know nothing about gangs," I said to him. "Can you tell me
a bit about how it's organized and why you would do what they
told you?"

"Okay," he said, and he began to tell me about his gang life and
taking orders. Greg said he and Mark were kind of rebellious and
unpredictable in the group, and he thought that the older gang
members were happy to have him run—also, because it would look
bad for himself if he got caught. He regretted listening to the gang
about leaving the murder scene and Mark's body. They knew he'd
end up imprisoned and out of their hair.

"You know, Greg, I was a bit nervous meeting you because I read
your file and there's quite a bit about all the violence in your family," I said. I picked up the file as I spoke, and I removed it from my
lap. "But I feel safe with you."

"Miss, I hear that a lot. I'm sure there's a lot of information in
that file, but I'm more than that," he said. He was referring to his
family file that included several male family members, who were or

had been in prison or mental institutions for murder. It was then that he stopped tapping his leg, and we continued to talk with no barrier between us.

On the day of the restorative justice circle, my co-facilitator and I drove to the Youth Detention Center compound. We were scheduled to meet everyone in a cement room, where we placed six chairs in a circle so we were all facing each other.

As usual, we left the center of the circle open, so that there was nothing physical between us. That open space is essential. It creates a sense of equality, access, and vulnerability among the participants. It's a very different atmosphere than what's created when one person sits behind a desk, on a pedestal, or on a stage.

I like to create an attractive space for restorative justice circles when I can, but after years of practicing restorative justice and talking circles in various locations, it's become clear to me that we can create a positive environment anywhere. What makes the real difference is not the aesthetics, but the quality of the interactions between us.

This particular circle came long after criminal charges had been filed, guilt was established, and Greg had begun serving the sentence imposed by the judge. This was a peacemaking circle, using established restorative justice principles of accountability, speaking from the heart, deep listening, and giving the victim of the offense an opportunity to be heard. This kind of sharing was vitally important to both Alan and Greg, who each loved Mark and grieved his death in their own way.

As facilitator, I started by saying that the caseworker and superintendent had approved the circle because they felt that Greg was ready emotionally and mentally, and that Greg had agreed to participate. I was aware that Alan had not attended the trial and had never met Greg before or after his son was killed. So I began by inviting Greg's case manager to talk about what Greg had been like when he entered detention, what he'd been doing at the center during his time there, and what he noticed about Greg's growth and maturity. He recalled a young boy full of attitude and rebelliousness, who masked his grief with a stiff upper lip. These days, the case manager recounted, Greg took other young, frightened, and angry boys "under his wing." He now showed an interest in learning skills and had developed a maturity that no one had expected.

Alan then shared with Greg how his life had changed since his son died. Alan recounted how he chose to work out-of-state and avoid New Mexico because of his son's death, specifically expressing his guilt over not being there to protect him, and his anger about what had happened.

"The hole in my heart is so painful, I can't bear it sometimes," Alan said. Finally, he asked Greg to tell him about that fateful day.

Greg took a deep breath. As he spoke, they both wept.

"First," Greg said, "I want you to know this was a terrible, stupid accident. We should never have been showing off with that gun. We never should have even had that gun. I miss Mark, too, you know. He was my *best* friend. We were together every single day. I never wanted to be at home, so I was at his house a lot, especially since his mom, your missus I guess, was usually out. So, we were goofing around, showing off to that girl who was there with us— waving that gun around and grabbing at it."

Greg continued, "Mark was really kind of dramatic, you know that, and he liked to horse around. It all happened so fast. I heard a loud pop, and then Mark was grabbing at his chest like in the movies, like he was shot, and I thought he was playacting. . . ."

Greg's voice got higher as he spoke, his words pouring out in a steady stream, as if he were pleading with Alan, desperate for him to see and understand his shock and horror as Mark lay dying.

"And then he moved his hand, and I saw the blood, and at first I thought, *Wow, how'd he manage to hide some ketchup or something to make it all look so real?* That was my first thought. I guess I never thought anything like this could really happen, and then I saw him just looking at me; he was astonished, too. And then he kind of just fell over, and before I even knew it his head was on my lap and that girl was crying and screaming and ran downstairs. And then she was back again and handed me the phone, and my lieutenant said, 'You just get out of there right now . . . right now. . . .'"

"I should have just stayed. Stayed there with him even though he wasn't breathing anymore. He was my best friend. You don't get many of them in life. At least, I haven't."

A deep silence filled the room once Greg stopped talking.

Alan thanked Greg for letting him know that his son hadn't died alone or been left to suffer. Then he asked Greg, "When are you getting out? And what do you plan to do next?"

Greg said he thought he should get far away from New Mexico—really fast—because Mark was a member of the same gang as he was, and they do not approve of killing fellow gang members. The room fell into silence again. Then, to everyone's surprise, Alan looked at Greg and put out his right hand, palm upturned in a gesture of offering. "I want to give my address to the superintendent to give to you when you are released." And then he turned to the superintendent and said, "Can you let me know when you release him? And give him this address?"

Alan went on: "You can stay safe by coming to stay with me in Alaska. There's a lot of work there for strong, young men. Please think about that. We don't have to keep talking about Mark; you've told me what I needed and wanted to know." Then Alan added, "Will you do that? Will you consider coming to where I am and see if it fits you?"

Greg nodded his head. Quietly, he said, "I will talk with my counselor. We'll talk about the options I have and when I decide what's best, I'll get in touch. Thanks for that."

With that exchange, I could sense a shared exhale of relief moving through the room. The kind of relief and calm that comes from communication that is honest and heartfelt. When one feels that "Yes, this is what was needed; the circle has been completed."

Every restorative justice circle needs to be closed in a dignified way. For me, gratitude is an essential component of dignity and closure. I expressed my gratitude for having witnessed this circle and thanked both men individually for their clear and direct communication. I invited Greg to shake Alan's hand. Then, one by one, each of us went around the circle with a word of thanks and a handshake. And so, our circle closed.

I am not authorized to follow a youth after his release, but I often think of Greg. I hope he is healthy and safe, whether in Alaska or elsewhere. I often think about what I witnessed in my preconference with him—how everything shifted and opened and became more human when we dropped our fears and our nervous defenses and instead met one another beyond the space of judgment. Honesty from the heart is what makes restorative justice a successful and effective process—one that can open a person's mind to the tragedy, suffering, and wide range of emotions that are part of our shared human experience. It's a process that can shift our perspective and grace the deepest pain with a healing touch.

Healing Sexual Assault Through Vicarious Restorative Justice

Dr. Joy von Steiger

I am a psychologist who has worked for thirty-five years with a diverse population of people who have suffered trauma. I am also a victim of sexual assault. I became interested in restorative justice after attending a retreat in a Massachusetts prison in 2017, organized by a group of incarcerated men who had developed a "vicarious" restorative justice program in their prison. Over that weekend, I sat in restorative circles with community members and incarcerated folks and witnessed the transformative power of these conversations to help the men—many of whom had committed murder—humanize their victims. Because their actual victims could not participate, the men had developed a program that used surrogate victims to help humanize both the people they had harmed and themselves. This vicarious approach allowed them to better understand the experiences in their lives that led them to make the devastating choices that ultimately brought them to prison.

When I was asked to co-facilitate a restorative justice circle for sex offenders, I initially said no. Too much personal trauma. Yet over the following few weeks, I kept thinking about restorative justice for sex offenders. Maybe I harbored a tiny hope I'd hear why they had committed their crimes and how those choices impacted them now. I needed to understand how someone can willingly choose to violently harm another human being. I finally agreed to join as a facilitator, but did not share that I was also a survivor; after all, I was a therapist, not a participant.

After that experience, I was hungry to learn more; I began to think that participating in a vicarious circle as a crime survivor might help me heal from my own trauma. I came across a 2021 Good Housekeeping *article about the work of Alissa Ackerman's Ampersands Restorative*

Justice, an organization that uses a vicarious restorative justice process with sexual offenders and survivors.[14] In a variation of the surrogate program I had seen in the prison, the Ampersands program paired a victim of sexual assault with the perpetrator of a comparable crime, allowing both to act as surrogates for each other.

I reached out to Alissa to ask if I could be a surrogate survivor for a person who had committed sexual harm. Several weeks after I committed to my own restorative process, Alissa called to tell me that I would be in a restorative conversation with Ben, a man who had sexually abused his children and served time for those crimes.

Throughout my childhood and young adulthood, I had been sexually abused and trafficked by family members, raped by their friends, assaulted by neighbors, strangers, and a babysitter. Female survivors of childhood sexual abuse are twice as likely to experience repeat assaults as women who have not experienced abuse. We learn that our bodies are not our own, and we are often not believed when we do tell adults of the harm we are enduring.

After I was raped when I was twelve, my uncle pulled me from his friend's car.

"You should be ashamed of yourself. That was disgusting."

I *was* ashamed, and I didn't need him to tell me it was my fault. It had to be my fault, or people I loved wouldn't keep doing this to me. Promiscuity, excessive use of drugs and alcohol, and depression reinforced my self-blame and loathing and masked my complex post-traumatic stress disorder. C-PTSD is a diagnosis given to people who have suffered chronic, long-term trauma and have additional symptoms such as suicidality, hopelessness, distrust of others, dissociative symptoms, and often chronic physical symptoms. Thirty-four years of therapy had barely touched my depression or C-PTSD. Different therapists, modes of therapy, antidepressants, antianxiety medicines, sleep medicines, massage therapy, and antipsychotics made little difference. Like many other survivors of sexual abuse, I blamed myself for the violence that was visited upon me. I didn't see myself as worthy of healing and care.

Ben and Alissa's team was located on the West Coast, and I was on the East. Alissa therefore scheduled a Zoom call to include me, Ben, Alissa, and her co-facilitator Sarah. (Ampersands was using Zoom to create more opportunities for restorative conversations to occur when distance and finances might preclude folks from participating.) Sarah, Alissa, and I met several times to discuss my goals, questions I had for Ben about his crime, and what I might need for support during what would be a Zoom call.

My friends were skeptical. They worried that I might be retraumatized by a manipulative con artist; they told me that they thought I was crazy to participate in this process. But my desire to feel whole again overrode those concerns.

The man who appeared on my computer screen had a thin, earnest-looking face, thinning brown hair, and sad, brown eyes. One of the first things I noticed about Ben was that he didn't look like anyone who had harmed me. I had decided before our meeting that if he looked like one of my abusers—maybe a similar haircut, glasses, or facial hair—I would call the whole thing off.

We began by sharing our "object of meaning," something we felt drawn to bring with us to our circle process. Ben pulled his object of meaning from his wrist—a bracelet of round brown beads, maybe nuts or seeds—and held it in front of him. I immediately noticed the little blue-green sea turtle among the brown beads. My breath caught in my throat as I remembered lying on the massage table thirty years earlier in a session with my bodyworker, Michelle, as she cradled my head and asked me to think of my animal guide in healing. I imagined myself lying on my back in the ocean with sea turtles swimming protectively around me. Sea turtles have since adorned my Christmas tree and desk; they have come to me at important points in my life to shepherd me into periods of clarity and growth.

"This was a gift from my mother. She's responsible for any good there is in me." He turned the bracelet over in his hands, his eyes glistening with tears.

I interrupted him, awed and eager to share our connection. "I chose a sea turtle as my animal guide while I was doing work on my trauma," I replied, as I felt my body unclenching. I shared my object of meaning, a small white stone on which my partner had painted a small red heart.

Sarah, one of our facilitators, asked me why I was there. I rustled through my notes, but my eyes wouldn't focus; neither would my brain. Why was I there? I was there because nothing else had worked. I was there because I didn't want to feel scared at night in my bed, because I didn't want to wake up, listening for an intruder. Because I didn't want to be constantly vigilant that my children might be harmed. I was there because I wanted to forgive, to see the good in people, and learn to love myself. That seemed like a lot to hope for from a two-hour meeting.

Instead, I said simply that I wanted to heal. Ben said that he wanted to continue to be accountable for the harm he caused his children by working toward my healing, which would be his penance of sorts. He was unable to have a healing conversation with his own children, as they had not spoken to him since he sexually abused them. In the interest of his own healing, he did everything he could to not bury the pain he caused his children.

Alissa and Sarah receded from view as I focused on Ben. He asked and I told him about the sexual violence I had experienced from my family and friends in my childhood, and how it kept happening. I told him about the loss of time with my children because of my deep depression and chronic PTSD—time I will never retrieve. I told him about numbing the pain with alcohol and promiscuity. I told him about loneliness, isolation, and a deep mistrust of men that made relationships hard to navigate. I opened up about the ever-present wish to die that I mostly keep to myself.

He cried for me and told me I didn't deserve to be treated that way. "You deserved to be protected. You deserved to be treated with care. None of what happened to you was your fault. I'm so sorry."

I felt seen, witnessed, valued. "Why did you do it?" I asked.

"I was in a bad place with drugs and alcohol. It isn't an excuse, it's the facts."

He was careful to say that his choices were his own. He wanted power over other people, to make them do what he wanted them to do; he wanted to be looked up to; he wanted to be loved. And so he sexually violated his children. He shared that, afterward, he wanted to die. Unable to keep his crimes a secret, he confessed to the police and then to his wife. He wanted his children to have help and healing immediately after he committed his crimes, regardless of the cost to him. He went to prison and lost his family, who he said never wanted to see him again.

"There isn't a day that goes by that I don't feel the impact of my choices and pray for my children's healing. It wasn't their fault. They loved me. I was sick."

And then: "I have devoted my life to healing myself, taking accountability and facilitating the healing of people who have been sexually harmed."

I left our session feeling that Ben was a compassionate man who made a devastating choice to sexually harm his children. Although I will never know his family's side of his story, I saw a disarming openness in his eyes as we spoke. I felt his appreciation for my pain, which he expressed by placing his hand on his chest while I shared my story in a state of emotional vulnerability, a gesture he repeated throughout our session. I felt gratitude for this man, who had committed to a process of healing for a stranger. As our time was coming to an end, I said to him, "Your mother did a good job."

His eyes brimmed with tears as he put his hand to his heart one last time. I did the same.

The session helped me to understand the heart of a perpetrator, which for so long had been a black box. They were not all monsters; they were people who made very bad choices that hurt people deeply and in ways that could not be completely mitigated. At the end of our meeting, I felt a calm and inner peace that I had never felt before: It was the feeling of freedom from self-hatred.

My life has changed immeasurably in the year since my surrogate victim-offender process. I was able to go off antidepressants successfully for the first time in thirty-four years. I have been able to develop a deep connection with a higher power, and to express deep gratitude for the blessings and gifts in my life. Participating in these restorative processes helped me to create an internal logic about my experiences as a survivor: that what happened to me was a *crime*. That I deserved to feel safe in my body. That I deserved compassion from myself and others. I can now love and grieve with a heart cracked wide open.

Alissa once told me in a follow-up conversation that healing comes in ripples. I see more possibilities for wholeness and healing as those ripples move across my horizon.

7.

Reconsidering Accountability in Prisons

Restorative circles are a growing practice within prisons, as a means of building empathy, self-reflection, and accountability among people who have committed serious harm. Many incarcerated people who engage in restorative circles recount that, in addition to eliciting empathy for those victimized by their crimes, the process has allowed them to confront and begin to heal from traumas that lie at the root of their harmful behavior. These programs are gaining favor among many criminal justice practitioners, including our storytellers, the Honorable Mary Triggiano and the Honorable Janine Geske—two former judges who have been bringing survivors of serious crimes to prisons to share the transformative power of restorative justice.

No Healing in Isolation

The Honorable Mary Triggiano

I am the director of Marquette Law School's Andrew Center for Restorative Justice. Before assuming that position, I was a judge for nineteen years, the last three years as chief judge of the Milwaukee County Circuit Court. The Andrew Center has been facilitating restorative justice circles at the law school and in the broader community for almost twenty-five years, beginning under the leadership of one of my former colleagues on the bench, Justice Janine Geske, retired director of the Andrew Center and distinguished professor of law.

My interest in restorative justice was ignited when, in 2007, Justice Geske invited me to participate in circles at the Green Bay Correctional Facility in Green Bay, Wisconsin. The experience was powerful—indeed, it was the catalyst to my learning more about restorative justice and implementing it throughout my time on the bench.

After leading dozens of restorative justice circles, I've seen true change in my participants when they realize that harm ripples through communities and touches everyone, even the harmdoer. During my nineteen years as a judge, I came to realize that our current justice system doesn't work for everyone. Those who are harmed and those who harm are often not set up for success to heal and overcome the countless challenges that they face after a crime has occurred.

As director of the Andrew Center, I practice and promote restorative justice with faculty and students and in the broader community, including through a Restorative Justice Clinic I teach that provides law students with experiential learning. We run many different programs, but I want to highlight our restorative justice healing circle at Racine Correctional Institution, in Sturtevant, Wisconsin—a medium-security state prison for men—because it truly exemplifies the transformative nature of restorative justice. Twice a year, law students and I facilitate an intensive, three-day trauma-sensitive and entirely voluntary circle at Racine with a group of around twenty incarcerated men. The objectives include: to promote generous listening, to see each other's points of view, to take ownership of acts they have committed, and to have empathy for each other's suffering. This is a tall order indeed in prison, where a defensive posture and tough exterior are considered essential modes of survival.

The supervisor at Racine with whom I collaborate closely is a true visionary. She believes that restorative justice is an essential tool to help people reflect on their mistakes, develop a greater sense of care toward others, and successfully reenter society. In other words, circles advance rehabilitation, the ostensible goal of our "corrections" system. In addition to first-time participants, she includes a few incarcerated men who have previous experience with restorative justice. These men are leaders in the prison—often serving lengthy sentences—who understand the transformative effect of circles and are working to embed a culture of restorative justice at Racine by helping their peers understand that sharing one's history and emotions in communion with others is both valuable and safe. I also invite law students from our clinic, three survivors of violent crime, and several community members from outside the prison.

Day One: Harm Is a Community Event

On the first day of the circle, I usually begin with a variety of prompts to build connection. I ask the participants to "tell us your first name and share one word about how you are feeling." Many of them answer "curious" or "tired." The incarcerated men are a little skeptical, unsure of what is going to transpire. The second prompt helps us learn more about each other. I ask everyone to "tell a story about a person who has significantly impacted your life and how." The men often talk about a deceased parent, grandparent, brother, or sister. Others talk about a friend who died from suicide or an overdose. A few mention someone waiting for them when they are released who will help them find a home and a job. You can see how participants' personal stories begin to resonate with others, already allowing for a deeper connection at a more human, interpersonal level.

Once our morning sharing is complete, we break for lunch. Upon return to our circle, I pose another prompt: "Describe an experience when you were affected by violence." It is a prompt that anyone can respond to, even if they were not a direct victim of violence. For the men at Racine, however, their experiences with violence are generally firsthand.

In one recent circle, this prompt elicited two and a half hours of sharing that centered on gun violence. Some men mentioned having scars from being shot. Others had been shot more than once. There were men who recently lost brothers or friends to gun violence and couldn't go to their funerals because they were incarcerated. There were men in the circle who had themselves shot people. Some were gang members who used guns to retaliate or protect turf.

One man held the talking piece with a stern face and stated, "I am a violent man. I committed a violent act which is why I am here. I lived in a violent neighborhood and learned to use violence at a young age." He stopped and passed the talking piece. We learned a lot about each other on the first day.

I often use team-building exercises to further connect participants and build trust. One of those exercises focuses on identifying the ripple effect of harm. We divide into groups to discuss the impact of a hypothetical armed robbery of a mom-and-pop grocery store during which the store owner falls and breaks his hip. By this point, group members quickly identify the harmful effects not only on the unfortunate grocer, but on his family, his employees, his customers, the neighborhood, the first responders, the families of the robbers, and even the robbers themselves. Later, participants in the circle begin to identify the ripple effects of harm they themselves had committed and harms they themselves had suffered.

Day Two: The Ecosystem of Harm

After the epiphanies of day one about the ripple effects of harm, we focus day two's conversation on the specific experience of people most impacted. The second day is centered on the incredibly painful stories of three courageous survivors of violent crimes who have agreed to serve as "surrogate victims" for the circle. They speak at length about their life; experiences before, during, and after being harmed; and about the toll the harm took on them and on their families. One of the survivors, Claude, shared an agonizing story about being shot in the face by a teenager during a carjacking. Another survivor, Penny, shared her experience of being brutally raped while on vacation with her family. Finally, Mayda described in detail how her son, Brian, was killed by a drunk driver while riding his bicycle.

Mayda and Penny have been telling their stories for almost twenty-five years now. They're the original storytellers from circles at the prison in Green Bay I first attended. They say that they find tremendous healing in the work they're doing, sharing their experiences with men in prison.

"I have received letters of understanding and support from many of the [men in prison] I came to know through participating in restorative justice circles in Wisconsin prisons," says Penny. She tells the participants that "much of my healing takes place because of men like you, I am not exaggerating!" She also offers one salient piece of advice to the men she meets in prison: "When we make a mistake, the best apology is how we live the rest of our lives."

At the end of day two, participants share their reaction to the survivors' stories. The impact on participants is real and palpable, as they begin to understand their role in an ecosystem of harm. There is no shortage of tears from community members, students, and the men. One of the men emphatically shared, "Listening to the stories today in circle, I am able to recognize a transformation within myself . . . but do we have the strength to remain faithful to what restorative justice means? Can we . . . do the hard and necessary work to repair the harm that we have caused? . . . I think we can." At the end of day two, everyone is emotionally exhausted, but there is a feeling of relief and deep connection.

Listening to the survivors almost always leads the men to remember the harms that they themselves had experienced through their lives, and the painful feelings or trauma associated with those events. In these sessions, all of us—community members, students, and survivors—come to realize that the majority of the incarcerated men were survivors of violent crimes of all sorts—including child abuse and sexual assault. Many witnessed domestic violence growing up. These reflections allow the participants and students to see that most people in prison were victims as well as perpetrators of violence, and that their experiences on both sides of harm have far-reaching ripple effects on themselves and their communities.

Day Three: A Circle of Healing at the Center

Day three focuses on healing harm to self and others. I ask, "What are we going to do after spending three powerful days with each other? How can we help make things right in our own lives for those we may have harmed?"

Many of the men had not slept much the night before; they were busy processing the survivors' stories and finding unique ways to express their emotions. As people pass the talking piece around, many participants acknowledge that they had never before considered the ripple effects of things they had done in the past, but that hearing from people who had been harmed by similar crimes stopped them in their tracks. That recognition was allowing them to own up to what they had done. Some of the men chose to share their feelings through creative means. One man wrote a gospel song and, after a bit of encouragement, sang it. Another wrote a rap song, got up in the middle of the circle, and performed it. Others wrote poems or created artwork.

One man wrote a four-page document because he said, "I can't just speak. I need to write and speak." He talked about the harm he committed and how he missed his family. He told us that "growing up I never expressed my feelings. My feelings and emotions, I always stuffed them and kept them to myself. But being able to be a part of this circle and meet you all hit different, and I am forever grateful for this moment. Restorative justice is power." As he read what he had written, occasionally he would stand and then sit back down. He did this repeatedly as he wiped away tears. He said, "When I stand, I cry less." In a response, every person in the circle rose to their feet to stand with him. We then sat down when he did. The outpouring of support was heartfelt.

The man who proclaimed on the first day that he was violent was excited to hold the talking piece on the third day. This time, he was smiling. In an animated voice, he said, "I called my wife last night and I said, 'Honey, go to Goodwill and buy a circle table. When I get out of here, I am going to go into my community. I'm going to put that circle table in the middle of the street, and I am going to have every young person and adult come and sit in circle with me. And we're going to talk about the ripple effect of harm, and we're going to talk about how violence is not the answer. Because if we continue to use violence to get back at somebody that's harmed us, we will end up in prison or dead. Our kids won't have a life.'"

He then declared that he was going to start a podcast so that people could learn more about restorative justice. I have seen him since that circle, on my frequent visits to Racine. He told me that his wife bought that table, and that she intended to start the project without him. He laughed and said, "She can't do that, because it's my idea and needs to wait for me." I know he wants to be part of the solution to the problem of violence occurring in his neighborhood. And I know he will, because he's now emotionally equipped to do so.

Day three also includes a skit designed to lead participants to identify and describe the positive effects of restorative justice. We divide into teams again and act out a skit where several people try to convince a person who deals drugs to participate in a restorative justice circle. Speaking as someone who played the role of the person dealing drugs, a law professor participant opined that the exercise not only summarized the restorative justice process and effects, but it also made everyone walk in someone else's shoes and look at the world from another perspective.

I ask one more question to close the circle. It is the same question I started with on day one: "How are you feeling?" The responses are different this time: "Excited." "Energized." "Hopeful." "Happy." One man who joins us each circle always says, "Love." As another community participant put it, "We are planting seeds of compassion, empathy, understanding, and healing." And even within the course of three days, we were able to see tiny sprouts emerge as the circle worked its magic. The Andrew Center continues to facilitate circles at Racine each semester to nurture those sprouts and plant more seeds of hope.

Epilogue: Ripple Effects

You might ask what happens after we leave the institution on the third day. What about the emotions that the circle has churned up? What about the trauma that surfaces? The program supervisor and I make sure the men have therapeutic supports after our sessions. The Andrew Center staff and students also return to Racine several weeks after each circle to check in on our participants to see how they are doing; community participants in the circle join, too, if they can. We also find that the Racine participants, having built deeper relationships among themselves, are ready to support each other in processing their emotions. After experiencing the transformative nature of a restorative justice circle, several of the men, with the program supervisor's help, are now organizing and facilitating their own small healing circles and have drafted a mission statement to guide their work. The mission statement names their goals as:

- Building upon and fostering community through the restorative justice circle experience.
- Actively engaging in trauma-informed practices.
- Acknowledging and addressing the impact our actions have on others, ourselves, and the community.
- Striving for healing, improvement of self, and restoration.
- Modeling self-accountability.
- Creating platforms for dialogue and healing.

In other words, they are striving to achieve through restorative justice a true rehabilitation and transformation of self, something that our current prison system rarely engages in. Many of the law students from our clinic who participate in the circle often speak of being transformed by this work as well. In a course evaluation at the end of the semester, one law student wrote, "It was incredible to see the immediate results restorative justice can have in bringing people together and the immense and necessary healing that occurs within the practice." A graduating law student said, "The lessons learned during this semester have fundamentally shaped my vision of what it means to be an attorney who fights for justice. It has not only enriched my legal education but has also instilled in me a deep commitment to promoting healing and reconciliation within our communities." I am always hopeful that the experience will be as meaningful to the law students as it has been for me; and that in their legal careers, they will use the skills they learned in our circle practice to reimagine and reshape our justice system to be more restorative, humane, and equitable.

Restorative justice works because it foregrounds collective healing and challenges the notion that violence is a behavior unique to certain individuals, when in reality many people are products of violent systems. Harm does not happen in a vacuum—and healing does not happen alone. In the years that I have been engaging in restorative justice with people in prison, I have come to believe that centering and supporting people who have been harmed—whether legally postured as an "offender" or a "victim"—is an important public safety and public health strategy. How we acknowledge harm and trauma can lead to healing and safety for survivors of harm; accountability and compassion for those who harm; stronger relationships; and safer communities.

When Knowing Is Healing

The Honorable Janine Geske

I started my career as a Legal Aid lawyer, later became a judge on the Milwaukee Circuit County Court, and then served as a justice on the Wisconsin Supreme Court for five years. I retired from the bench to join Marquette University Law School, where I directed the university's Andrew Center for Restorative Justice. In this role, I worked with the Catholic Church on cases of clergy abuse and have gone into maximum security prisons to do circles with people incarcerated there. I have also facilitated victim-offender dialogues in severe crimes.

Over my career, I've seen the limitations of an adversarial process of justice. But when I was a judge presiding in homicide cases and heard about restorative justice, I thought, That is the craziest, nuttiest, left-wing liberal thing I've ever heard. I can't imagine why a victim or surviving family member would want to sit down across a table from someone who had done them harm. . . .

The story of my very first victim-offender dialogue proved me wrong.

This story is about a young fellow named Jack, eighteen years old, who called a Chinese restaurant for take-out delivery to a house where he knew no one was home. The house was dark, and Jack was hiding in the bushes when Tim, the delivery man from the restaurant, arrived. Jack had a gun. Jack later said that his intention was to hold the delivery man up and demand his money; he did not plan to shoot him. But when he held the gun to Tim's head, the gun went off accidentally. Tim was killed. He left behind an elderly father and two daughters. Jack was convicted of murder and sentenced to prison for a lengthy term.

About seven years later, Tim's two grown daughters decided that they wanted to meet with Jack. They wanted to share with him the devastation he had caused their family. The case was assigned to me at the Andrew Center for Restorative Justice.

For more than six months, I met with all of the parties on numerous occasions to prepare them for meeting each other. During our pre-meetings, I learned how one of Jack's daughters, Carol, lived in terror for months and months because she thought it might have been a gang shooting. She wondered whether they were going to come into her house and continue their killing. "Every time I went into my house, I would look in all my closets and under the bed," she recounted. She slept with the lights on for years. "That fear existed for so long," she said.

Her sister, Margaret, had been a recovering alcoholic at the time of their father's death and relapsed from the stress. She wound up having a car accident and going to jail herself as a result. The sisters also shared how their grandfather (Tim's father), who was elderly, used to love to golf with his son. After Tim was murdered, his dad never went golfing again. He died on the one-year anniversary of his son's death.

These were consequences of the murder that Jack wouldn't have known about, because they occurred after his sentencing hearing, but the sisters felt that he should know the short- and the long-term impact his actions had on them and their family. But they also wanted to hear Jack's version of what happened. They had heard through third parties that he said it happened "accidentally." But they wanted to hear it in his own words. Finally, Carol and Margaret wanted to ask him questions about his life: Why did he have a gun, and how he had gotten to this place of taking a life? Things that only he could answer.

They also had another nagging question: Had their father fallen face first or on his back when he was shot? This would not be the

last time I had heard such a question from a homicide family survivor, even though a person might think that odd. Why would a
grieving person want to know that kind of detail?

My experience with surviving family members of homicide is
that the small details are so important. They replay the death over
and over in their heads, and at some point, some of them want to
know exactly what transpired. In prep meetings, I have sometimes
asked survivors, "What if the answer is really horrible?" And survivors always tell me the same thing: "He [or she] has already done
the worst to me. I want to know exactly how it happened."

When I met with Jack, I learned that he had been a model pris-
oner for the most part. He didn't have a significant criminal record
before this crime, and he was actually eager to have the meeting.
Jack really wanted Tim's family to hear that he did not intentionally kill their father.

When we were finally ready to have the face-to-face meeting,
emotions were running high.

The first thing we do as we meet together is to lay the ground-
work. We create a safe environment for everyone present. In homicide cases like this one, we always hear from the surviving family
first. We start by talking about the person who died. Who was
Tim as a father? What did it mean to lose their dad in this violent
way? We typically bring an 8×10 photograph of the victim, because
often the offender never actually had a good look at the person and
certainly didn't know him. This was true of Jack. So the sisters had
an opportunity to introduce their father to Jack, and to share with
him everything that had transpired from the funeral onward.

It is always very moving—and often devastating—for an
offender to listen to that. As a trial lawyer and later as a judge,
I've sat through hundreds and hundreds of felony sentencings in
courtrooms. I can tell you that in a courtroom, there is never an

appropriate opportunity for a victim to tell those intimate kinds of details to an offender.

In many states, victims are given an opportunity to make or read a victim impact statement in court. In those statements, an offender might hear that it was a terrible crime, and that it was awful for the family. But in a court hearing, you don't hear what the funeral or the cemetery was like, or what happened in the year after. You don't hear how people suffer on the anniversary of a loved one's death. In all the cases I've done or presided over in a regular justice process, I have yet to see an offender—male or female—look as if they have been deeply moved by what was said in a courtroom, even though by that time they've either admitted guilt or been convicted of the crime. The offender, first of all, has been told by their lawyer, "Don't look at the victim." Usually, the best a crime survivor can get from an offender in a courtroom is, "I'm really sorry," or "I wish it were me instead." But victim-offender dialogues are always deeply moving.

Carol and Margaret then asked Jack about his upbringing. They wanted to know what he had been doing in prison. Typically, one of the surviving family members wants to know if there is still risk to other people if the offender is ever released. All those kinds of questions.

Jack told his story about how he'd needed money, how he'd set the crime up, and where he got the gun. Even though during our preparation, I had prepared Tim's daughters for the kinds of things they would hear, it was still difficult for them. Jack's expression of remorse was much more profound after he'd heard Carol and Margaret talk, and he was obviously very moved by them.

This is generally the moment when we see a turning of the energy in the room, often referred to as when the "heart shift" happens. It is meaningless to victims for the most part to hear expressions of remorse in the courtroom, because it doesn't sound sincere. But it is so much more powerful after an offender has heard, in great detail, during an extended face-to-face conversation, what a victim has to say. Jack was deeply moved, and it is totally different from hearing "I'm sorry" in a courtroom for a victim to see an offender's genuine response. That is what happened for Carol and Margaret. They saw exactly how affected Jack was by what they were telling him.

At one point, Carol asked a question we often hear from survivors: "What do you do on the anniversary of the homicide? We can tell you what we do. We go to the grave site." Jack responded, "I am very cognizant of that date. I know the date is coming around. I know what time of the day it happened. Sometimes I'm supposed to go to class; I won't go to class that day. And I don't sleep well." You can imagine what Carol and Margaret had envisioned. They thought after his sentencing he was sitting in a nice cell somewhere and watching TV. Hearing that the crime impacted him emotionally made a difference for them.

I often ask the person who's committed the crime, "Do you have questions? Are there things you want to ask?" Jack said, "No, I'm just here to answer their questions to help them through this. I'm not going to ask any questions." This encouraged Carol and Margaret to share more intimate details with Jack, including a very interesting story about their dad.

Tim closely followed the New York Yankees, and so his family decided they wanted to inscribe the Yankees' logo on his tombstone. But the tombstone company said they couldn't do that without permission from the team. Carol and Margaret wrote a letter to the Yankees and told them the story of their father's murder, and the Yankees allowed it. So they buried their dad with the New York Yankees insignia on his tombstone.

You can imagine that by this time, the chill in the room was gone. There was a warmth, there was listening. I've seen this in other dialogues as well: After we have gotten through all the really tough discussions, people naturally try to find a connection with each other.

It might sound kind of crazy, but it's similar to when you go on vacation far away, and you meet somebody there from your hometown. If I go to Europe and see somebody with a Wisconsin sweatshirt, I tend to want to go talk to them and see if they know anybody that I might also know. It's a little ridiculous, because in Wisconsin I certainly wouldn't start that kind of conversation.

But that is exactly what happened right there in the prison. The exchange went from, "Let's talk about this murder" to "Did we have some connection when we were younger?" And it turned out that all three of them had grown up in the same community.

Two remarkable things then happened. One sister went over and gave Jack a big hug. She said how appreciative she was that he was willing to meet her. Jack thanked them for being willing to talk to him and to listen to him. The other sister was closely connected to her church; for her, the dialogue was an important part of her faith journey. She didn't share it there, but she told me afterward that she had not been able to bear hanging her father's picture on the wall since the day of his murder. But that after this meeting with Jack, she put it up.

This was my first victim-offender dialogue in a homicide case. It was breathtaking.

But there's another miracle in this story. As I said earlier, Carol and Margaret wanted to ask Jack whether their dad had fallen face forward or face up. They did ask Jack that question. He said, "The gun went off and I ran. I really didn't see, so I don't know how he fell."

The session was over. We left the prison, and I drove Carol and Margaret back to their home in Racine. I had a class at the law school I was teaching that night, on evidence. It had nothing to do with restorative justice, but I was so hyped about our victim-offender dialogue that I asked Carol, Margaret, and Jack whether it was all right for me to share parts of their story with students. All three said yes, but Margaret cautioned, "Don't give any identifying information because our brother does not know that we're doing this, and we don't want him to find out."

I went to my class. There were about 60 students in the class. When I spoke to them about it, I didn't mention the exact scene or the specific facts around the homicide itself. But I talked about some of the incredible moments we had, including how the sisters shared with the man who killed their father the story of putting the Yankees' insignia on his tombstone. One young man came up to me after class and said, "I heard it happened in Racine."

I thought, *Oh God*, and I felt awful, thinking that I had betrayed the family's trust. I said, "Well, but it's really important that nothing be said." But he named the victim and asked if it was that case.

And now I was feeling even worse. So immediately I reiterated to him that it was really important that this story not be shared with anyone. As I was gathering my papers, this man was starting to walk out of the classroom. I thought to myself, *I still don't know why he knows about this case*. And so I ran after him.

I asked him, "Did you recognize the tombstone story?" I thought maybe he was from Racine, and that he heard that somewhere. He said, "No." And I said, "So how did you know about this?"

He answered, "I used to be a Racine police officer. I was the first officer on the scene that night, before even the paramedics arrived."

I was stunned. I looked at him and said, "Do you by any chance remember if the man was face up or face down on the ground?" And he said, "Yeah, he was face up."

I called Carol and Margaret two hours later, and I said, "I have the answer to your last question."

Now, what are the odds of anything like that happening? It still gives me chills. Yet, I've seen a number of fortuities like that in the years that I have been facilitating victim-offender dialogues. Margaret, who was more religious than Carol, just said, "That was a sign from God."

Since that time, Carol and Margaret stayed in touch with Jack. They appeared at every parole hearing he had since our dialogue, and they watched his progress. Margaret began volunteering with a prison ministry. And eventually at one of his parole hearings some years later, after he had served a substantial sentence, they both stood up and said they thought Jack should be paroled. Carol and Margaret now talk publicly about their restorative justice experience with Jack as transformational. He was paroled with the support of the sisters. The last I heard he was doing well in the community.

I see the transformative power of restorative dialogues for other homicide survivors regularly. In one case I facilitated, an intoxicated driver ran a red light and killed a young woman who attended the same university he did. At the dialogue with the parents and sister of the victim, they shared a video depicting her life, made for our session: photographs of her as a baby, a video of her baptism and her first communion, then birthday parties and Christmases. As the film screened, the tears were just streaming down the young man's face. I mean, just quietly crying and crying. I looked over at the victim's sister, who had to this point been so angry that she had not been able to speak. She looked over at him, reached down into her purse and passed him a tissue to wipe his tears.

She never said, "I forgive you." It's not necessarily about that. But it was a moment of release. And when we walked out, all three of the victim's family members hugged him. The sister was the last one to leave, and as she did, she said to him, "You've just changed my life today." Some of that rage and anger had dislocated when she was able to see and experience his sincere sorrow and remorse.

This is the unique gift of restorative justice for survivors of serious crime: It offers them a way to release some of their pain and anger in a meaningful exchange with the person who harmed them, in a way that a courtroom process is just not designed to give.

Part Four

Community Harms

8.

Hate Crimes

Because they are intended to induce fear and terror in an entire sub-set of people, hate crimes create harm that is far-reaching, even when the physical act (spray painting hateful graffiti, for example) might otherwise constitute a minor violation. While sentencing laws today enhance penalties for hate crimes, a regular justice process can punish harmdoers severely without ever requiring them to con-front or comprehend the impact of their actions. In these cases, a restorative justice process enables those harmed to educate an offender on the repercussions for their community. As stories in this chapter demonstrate, plans for repair in crimes of bias often require perpetrators to learn about and engage directly, through acts of service, with the community they have impugned. Because form-ing relationships with people across lines of difference is the best antidote to prejudice, outcomes here can be far more effective than traditional forms of punishment.

Real Relationships, Real People, Real Dialogue

Ted Lewis

When Saudi terrorists attacked the United States on September 11, 2001, many people worried what danger might come next. But for Arab Americans, there was an additional set of concerns: "Will there be reprisals against us?" they immediately wondered. And, indeed, Muslims and people who appeared to be Arab suffered numerous threats and acts of violence in the weeks that followed.

In the midst of these negative repercussions throughout the country, a surprisingly positive opportunity to address an anti-Muslim hate crime emerged in the Bethel neighborhood of Eugene, Oregon. The local district attorney referred a case to a new Community Accountability Board that was operating in conjunction with the Restorative Justice Program of Community Mediation Services (now called the Center for Dialogue and Resolution). The assistant to the district attorney was a strong restorative justice advocate; she had played a key role with me in developing the neighborhood pilot project. I managed the restorative justice program and oversaw the fledgling accountability board.

The following account presents a restorative justice intervention that was mobilized very quickly to address a disturbing and hurtful crime in a way that brought significant equilibrium back to those who were most involved.

Two hours after the first of the Twin Towers of the World Trade Center collapsed on 9/11, the Islamic Cultural Center in Eugene, Oregon, received a phone call. "All of you Muslims should be erased from our society!" said a male voice. Palestinian-born Tammam Adi, who directed the center, was on the receiving end of that message, which was laced with profanity. Soon after, the same man made a second call to the local mosque and left a similar death threat on the answering machine.

Well before this time, Tammam was already grieved by the constant coupling of the word "Islamic" with terms like "extremist, radical," or "terrorist" in the media. He understood how this form of messaging was intensifying stereotypes in the minds of most Americans. And now, in the wake of 9/11, he and other Muslims in the United States feared reprisals and legitimately worried for their physical safety.

The local police were able to trace the calls to a middle-aged man named Chris and apprehended him later that same day. They learned that Chris was not acting as a representative of a local hate group, but rather was acting independently. Still, Tammam and his wife Pat contacted the local Human Rights Commission to request their help and protection. Police protection was also provided at their home for that first week.

"We don't want to look vindictive in court," Tammam and Pat explained as they discussed legal options with the district attorney and Human Rights Commission staff. When they learned that there was a community-based alternative that prioritized facilitated dialogue over a contested process, they gave a sigh of relief. Being involved in a court trial process made them feel more vulnerable to public scrutiny and potential further attacks. Restorative justice was new to them but aligned with their values and instincts about resolving harms and conflicts humanely.

Tammam and Pat expressed their willingness to engage in a dialogue process with the responsible party, and Chris also told the prosecuting attorney of his willingness to apologize and make amends. Sometimes this is viewed as an "easy way out" for offenders, to avoid a formal sentence in a criminal court. However, a restorative process has built-in safeguards, with preparation meetings to assess people's motives and minimize the potential for survivors of harm to be revictimized.

When the case was formally referred to our mediation agency, I became the lead facilitator working alongside two other volunteers. The first of several preparatory meetings with Chris happened within a week of September 11. In this meeting he described how he acted out of rage when he first heard the news of the towers coming down. He blamed Muslims and wanted to scare those who were living in his vicinity.

What was surprising to us, though, was that Chris was already expressing remorse for his actions. He admitted to a long history of anger problems, which had built up over the years. He knew that he needed to get counseling but had never taken that step. He related an interesting synchronicity that had occurred just a few hours before he came to his initial meeting with our team. When he opened the phone book to find the number to call for a possible counselor, he turned to the very same page where he had found the number for the mosque. A jolt of insight overcame him. "I went to the very page looking for help that I went to in order to create the problem."

A routine aspect of initial meetings with harming and harmed people is to just listen to their story. What did you experience? What has it been like for you since then? Another common element is to inform them about what makes a restorative process distinctive, such as understanding the importance of repairing harm rather than punishment. Facilitators also tune into the needs and preferences of all participants. Chris had stated early on his wish to apologize in person to the Islamic leader and his family; he wanted to show that he was a better person than his actions may have suggested. "I'd like a peaceful solution," he added.

A week later, our facilitator team met with Tammam and Pat, along with the director of the Human Rights Commission. Tammam spoke of the way the phone call impacted him. Amazingly, he had tried to reason with the caller, saying, "Maybe we should wait to see who really did it." But when the caller continued his threatening speech about death to all Muslims, Tammam hung up. He straightway feared retaliation and felt very vulnerable, like a "sitting duck." In the Middle East, death threats are taken very seriously. He described feeling frozen with fear and uncertainty.

Central to Tammam's concerns was the caller's motive: "Why did he do it to us?" He expressed interest in meeting with the offender so he could hear him say why he did it and, hopefully, why he wouldn't do it again.

Pat also had much to share regarding how she was affected. Along with many other Muslim women, in the wake of the 9/11 attacks she had stopped wearing the hijab, the traditional Muslim scarf, around her head. Threats were coming very close to home. A boy had approached their daughter at her high school and said, "We should round up all the Muslims and shoot them." Fortunately, the Adi family was also surrounded during these frightful days by local people who were expressing support and solidarity. And police protection followed them wherever they went.

The facilitators held one additional preparatory meeting with both parties before scheduling a first joint dialogue meeting on October 10, just a month after the national tragedy. These meetings focused on helping the parties prepare themselves for what they might say and how they might respond to each other's statements. We were also able to manage expectations and explain which other stakeholders would also be present at this meeting.

The first of two restorative conferences took place in the Bethel neighborhood in northwest Eugene. Community members from the Bethel Accountability Board attended the meeting, all of whom had some previous training or orientation in restorative processes. Also present were the prosecuting attorney, the assigned police officer, a representative from the Human Rights Commission, and the assistant district attorney and probation officer who helped to launch the project.

I had set the room up in a large circle to represent communal equality and investment in the process. But this was not a formal circle with a talking piece and go-around prompts. This was a facilitated dialogue that allowed for more open discussion and gradual trust building. As lead facilitator, I knew that Tammam was not comfortable being in a position where Chris would be straight across from him and able to make eye contact. So, I had them sit on either side of our facilitator team.

With over two dozen people present, it was also important that both parties had side rooms where they could wait ahead of time with their support people. It can be hard to adjust in a meeting that involves lots of emotion when you just show up in a room bustling with people. Each side room also had one facilitator there.

Given that this meeting was occurring mere weeks after 9/11, everyone in the room was feeling emotions ranging from anger about the first foreign attack on American soil since Pearl Harbor to fear for their own safety. The meeting took over two hours and was marked by a fair degree of emotional tension. I made some introductory statements that acknowledged the unique aspects of this case in light of the terrorist attack. I emphasized that repairing the harm of destructive words that emanated from a larger act of terrorism would require constructive dialogue.

About halfway through the meeting, I could tell that both the Adis and the community board members were not satisfied with Chris's answers to their questions. He had apologized early on, but some of them doubted his sincerity. The stakes were also high, for Chris knew that if this process did not succeed, the prosecuting attorney—who was seated near the door in the back of the room— was prepared to charge Chris formally and route the case to a court proceeding. Chris felt overwhelmed by all the questions coming at him and the pressure from the community members, some of whom had law enforcement backgrounds. At the same time, community members were also conveying to Chris their desire for a meaningful process of reintegration, in addition to accountability.

At one point, someone pointed out that Tammam was not able to make eye contact with Chris. Tammam openly acknowledged this was so. He explained that in Palestinian culture, making eye contact with an adversary meant certain things, and to play it safe, you avoided eye contact. Tammam seemed even more fearful and vulnerable than during our preparation meetings.

At about the two-hour mark, an important thing happened. Pat declared that the conversation felt "stuck"—what I call the lack of good "heart shift." Even better, she recommended that we all take a two-week break and commit to coming back for a second meeting. This would allow Chris to have time to meet with a new counselor he had found and to address some of the patterns of anger he alluded to during the meeting.

After everyone else had left the room, Chris remained behind to chat with me alone. He talked more openly about his apprehensions about the meeting and how he was feeling under fire. He knew folks meant well, but the large number of people in the room speaking and asking questions was a lot for him to deal with. It made me question my own decisions regarding how I had structured the meeting, especially regarding the number of people involved. And yet I knew that everyone wanted to see this process through to a good end.

What really opened things up in that one-on-one was when Chris confided how hurt he felt when one of the community members had said, "You shouldn't be raising a child with your anger issues and racial prejudice." I knew from our prep meetings with Chris that he had lost a twenty-month-old son after a failed surgery. That baby boy, he now explained, died on September 14, 1995. Every year, when September rolled around, Chris struggled more acutely with anger and depression. Upon learning this, I encouraged Chris to share this part of his story in the next conference meeting. "It might help folks to make better sense of your situation," I suggested.

As the two intervening weeks unfolded, I stayed in close contact with both parties. There was time for debriefing and time to consider what people most needed from a second meeting. Chris kept coming back to fear of loss. He didn't want this process to end up being another experience of loss. I advised him to lean into the future and manage only what was in his control. "You can focus on making amends and improving your life," I said. "That's enough for now."

Meanwhile, the Adis benefitted from the time out to crystalize the questions they still wanted answered: Did Chris act alone or as a member of a racist group? Was this his first hateful act, or part of an ongoing pattern? What went on in his mind between seeing the news of the terrorist act and picking up the phone? They were also able to sharpen their requests for restitution and reparation. At bottom, Tammam and Pat just needed Chris to go further and deeper to account for why he did it.

During one of these conversations, Tammam asked what I thought was the most important thing to address in the upcoming meeting. I said, "Since it might be difficult for Chris to fully account for his actions psychologically and socially, it would be helpful if our conversation included a mutual agreement with clear, achievable goals." I suggested that we use the first hour to talk about lingering concerns related to the hate call and then use the second hour to reach some sort of solution. "If we don't shift from the past to the future, folks can stay discouraged."

On October 30, the full group came back together for the second joint conference. I proposed we first complete the discussion from two weeks earlier about the offense itself and then consider reparations in the last hour of our two-hour meeting. This time, a reporter from the region's primary newspaper was present. I explained that the reporter was there "off the record," but would likely be involved in follow-up interviews and future coverage. Eventually, a couple of stories were written up in the Eugene *Register-Guard*.

The community members opened with a brief discussion of their expectations of residents in their neighborhood, and the impact of the crime on the community. Chris was then invited to give an update on his progress with counseling, his family, and his job. He mentioned that he had told his employer about the whole situation, which impressed the victims. But the most important thing he brought up was the account of his infant son's death six years earlier, explaining how this anniversary triggered his trauma every September. With Tammam sitting close to my side, I could sense that this information about Chris's loss helped connect some dots between his past pain and his misdirected rage.

Tammam responded by asking Chris a string of new questions. These didn't feel pressuring or accusatory; it was a line of inquiry intended to get to the heart of things. Chris did his best to answer each one in turn. This is the sort of spontaneous exchange that can be inhibited if circle processes rely too strictly on go-around prompts.

"I'm satisfied with what I have heard," Tammam said in response. "I think we can move forward." A palpable shift took place in the room. As often happens in restorative conversations where people both listen deeply and are deeply heard, the tensions that mark the start of meetings were transformed into a lighter, more optimistic mood. When "heart shift" happens, it allows people to move forward to discuss future terms of coexistence.

After a short break the group began to discuss options for reparation. The Adis asked for a public letter of apology to the Muslim community. Later it was agreed that this could be printed in the *Register-Guard* as a letter to the editor. They also wanted Chris to attend two upcoming lectures on the religion of Islam. "Everyone knows Muslim stereotypes, but nobody knows about the religion of Islam," Tammam once told me.

After further discussion, three more agreements were added: Chris would cooperate in news coverage of the case, commit to continue his counseling, and speak to teens in juvenile detention about his experience. A concern was raised that Chris's new job might be jeopardized by the press coverage. Tammam said that if it came to that, he would personally talk to the employer to help Chris keep his job. Chris was moved by this but simply said that he was willing to accept any consequences for his actions. The assistant district attorney created a written document that was signed by all parties.

A highlight for me personally came at the close of the meeting. Before everyone left the circle, Tammam unexpectedly approached Chris, reaching out his arm to shake Chris's hand. It was a moving gesture that spoke of the progress the two parties had made. In fact, after this, everyone got up and began shaking hands with one another in good spirits, buoyed by the sense of relief and reconciliation in the room.

In the weeks that followed, Chris attended the two lectures on Islam that Tammam recommended. At the first lecture, he was met by Tammam at the door. Inside, Chris sat next to Pat in the front row. He later told me that he had enjoyed being there, had learned a lot, and was motivated to attend additional lectures on his own.

Chris's letter of apology was printed on the editorial page of the *Register-Guard* on November 18, 2001, alongside a front-page account of the crime and its reparation through restorative justice. When it came time later that winter for Chris to speak at the youth detention center, I accompanied him and was impressed with how he told his story with authenticity, and how the youth listened with curiosity and good questions.

A number of things aligned well in order to make this a successful restorative process. First, the district attorney and human rights office involved bought into the notion of restorative justice as an alternative to a criminal prosecution. From the outset, the harmed party preferred a community-supported dialogue process over a court-based experience. The responsible person was remorseful early on and took full ownership for his actions. The community, in partnership with justice agencies, already had a collaborative mechanism through which to quickly mobilize a responsive process for this type of hate crime.

I also believe that this case had a wider and more symbolic impact, beyond the healing it offered the three directly impacted parties. As the whole city of Eugene was reeling from the events of September 11, 2001, this restorative story shined a light of hope in the midst of a darkening world. It allowed a grieving community to play a cathartic role in healing harm that emanated from the tragic events of that day.

When a Joke Isn't a Joke

Trudy Junkroski

Despite perceptions to the contrary, a restorative conference process requires courage on the part of everyone who says "yes" to participating. As a voluntary process, anyone involved can choose to walk away when the going gets rough, allowing the case to be handled through the court or other means. Restorative conferences are for the courageous—those who are willing to face one another, sit with uncomfortable emotions, speak honestly, listen deeply, and work together to find a way forward.

One such courageous group of people gathered in response to a crime committed in their community of 36,000 residents, located just outside of New York City. Late one night, four high school students spray painted racist and antisemitic graffiti on a prominent bridge in the town, alarming residents, stirring up fear and questions about hate and bias within the community. The boys identified by police as responsible were all minors, except for one. Having just turned eighteen, that young man was facing criminal charges for his actions. The district attorney's Hate Crimes Unit referred the matter to our agency, wondering if there might be an opportunity for the community to be involved in addressing the harm.

Eventually, a restorative conference was convened with the oldest young man, his family, and several other community members willing to participate. People from the town who volunteered to speak about the impact of the incident from their perspective included an educator and racial justice advocate, along with a rabbi, and one other member of the Jewish community.

The restorative conference occurred with the group seated together in a synagogue, speaking about what happened and how they were impacted, asking questions, expressing their concerns and love for their community. Together, with the young man's input, the group developed a plan for how he could begin to repair the harm and ease the fears of his community. While I am obliged to keep the details of the conference confidential, as promised to the participants, the young man later wrote about his experience of meeting with the group and the impact it had on him, which I have permission to share here.

Last June, I was one of the students involved with spray painting offensive language on a highway underpass. I wanted to apologize for all the distress this incident caused and recognize that there is no acceptable explanation for what was done.

In the months since, I've been working hard to understand what led me to that moment. As I have been picking up the pieces of my own life, I want to share what I've learned, in hopes that it might help other kids in the future from making the same terrible mistake.

First, I learned that words of hate can actually hurt people. Words have power, and the words that were written have a history, but the hurt happens in the present. This might sound obvious to everyone, but it wasn't to me. I've heard all the speeches in school about racism and antisemitism being wrong, and I've been to the Holocaust Museum and Museum of African American History in Washington, DC. I'd been told it was wrong, but it seemed like a history lesson and not something that still impacted people today.

If I were to tell you that what happened that night was meant to be a kind of joke, would you believe me? I knew we didn't mean it. I knew we weren't racist or antisemitic. We were just being stupid kids, we thought. We lived in a wealthy suburb with plenty of privilege, not a lot of accountability, and absolutely zero experience with being on the receiving end of discrimination or hate.

Through my healing journey I learned that people in the local African American and Jewish communities who thought something like this would never happen in their small town, realized it could. One temple in our town showed me the new security system they'd installed after hearing about the spray paint. This incident had cultivated fear in their hearts. The security system is designed to listen for gunshots and is always on. One African American family in my neighborhood told me this wasn't the first time something like this happened, and in their opinion, it wouldn't be the last. They appreciated that I talked to them, but had little hope that anything would change.

I'd like to tell you that all that needs to be done to prevent other kids from doing this is more education; an assembly at school from someone important and the problem is solved. But like I wrote earlier, I'd been to those. I was that kid who listened but didn't really hear. Instead I've been taking a diversity course, one-on-one, really trying to get into the background of how a kid like me could have such a casual perspective about hate speech. If I'd truly understood the power of hate speech, I wouldn't have been able to take part. The teacher I've been working with has covered only three topics so far and overall I have spoken with him for a total of nine hours, and I feel like I have only scratched the surface.

I guess my point is that there is no easy fix. But here are some ideas: education that really challenges kids, connects history to challenges in their own lives or family or community; getting on top of mental health challenges; learning about privilege and accountability. There is no shortcut. It takes time.

I have done a lot of growing up in the last six months and still have a lot of growth ahead. I am working to find a valuable role in my family and community so that not only do I not make this kind of mistake ever again, but that it would be inconceivable. As my diversity teacher told me, if I'd understood the power of hate speech, I wouldn't have taken part in the first place. My hope is that some kid reading this story thinks twice before saying or writing something offensive. Think about it three times, four times, even five, because the impact of your actions can be much more serious than you can possibly imagine. Again, words have power and can cause harm.

Through the restorative process, the overwhelming amount of reality I was being hit with as I was listening and digesting what everyone was saying made it that much more impactful for me. It was like the mask of ignorance had been removed and my eyes were open to actions and consequences, and understanding.

Restorative Justice as an Atonement

Fred Van Liew

Over the course of my career, I've been a lawyer, mediator, facilitator, community organizer, trainer, and consultant. Today, I direct the Cumberland County Friends of Restorative Justice in Portland, Maine, and manage Restorative Practice Associates in Portland and Des Moines, Iowa.

For most of my twenty-eight years as a practicing attorney, I worked as a prosecutor "inside the system," retiring in 2010. From experience, I can say that we can do much better when it comes to our response to crimes and those who commit them.

The following story, from my early years as a prosecutor, recounts a restorative dialogue between members of a Jewish congregation and two young people who desecrated their temple with antisemitic slogans.

Members of the Temple B'nai Jeshurun woke on a Saturday morning to find neo-Nazi graffiti scrawled on the side of their synagogue. Initially, there were no suspects, but there was anger and outrage. At one level, the incident was a galvanizing experience, bringing together the broader religious community in a way never witnessed in Des Moines. At another, however, it brought forth shadows normally hidden within many good and well-intentioned people; some cried out for a justice like that sought by vigilantes and lynch mobs.

Two weeks later, an eighteen-year-old male and a seventeen-year-old girl—boyfriend and girlfriend—were arrested for the crime and charged with felony mischief. I was a senior prosecutor at the time the case came in; I held on to it rather than assigning it to a line prosecutor, because I had a notion that we might be able to manage this case differently.

I called Steven Fink, the rabbi at Temple B'nai Jeshurun, asking how he was doing, and how members of the temple were doing. He told me he was angry, and that others were angry and afraid. I asked if he had ever heard of restorative justice and then described its potential for healing. I asked if he would consider meeting with the young offenders.

He said my description of restorative justice made sense to him, and that it was consistent with his religious tradition, but in this instance, he thought that neither he nor temple members would consider meeting the offenders. I thanked him for his time, gave him my number, and encouraged him to call if he had questions. A week later, he did.

Rabbi Fink told me there had been much discussion following our phone conversation. He said there were some temple members who saw the wisdom of a meeting, while others felt a meeting would be used to minimize the harm done and would result in the offenders receiving just a slap on the wrist. But in the end, a consensus was reached that the temple should go forward with a meeting, even in the face of uncertainty and possible revictimization. It was agreed that an evening meeting would take place at the synagogue. The people representing the temple would be the rabbi, two Holocaust survivors who had gone into hiding following the graffiti desecration of the synagogue, a former member of the Israeli army, and three temple elders. The young offenders would be accompanied by their attorneys. I would be present in my role as prosecutor, and an experienced mediator would facilitate the conversation.

The evening came. We found ourselves seated around a large conference table at the synagogue. Low lighting and centerpieces made of candles and flowers set a tone appropriate for the seriousness of the gathering. Following the requisite introductions, an explanation of the process, and the signing of a confidentiality agreement, the stories began.

They flowed out—hesitatingly at first, and then in a rush, with tears, anger, and fear. Old memories were resurrected. Details of childhood nights in concentration camps rose to the surface. Stories were told of the struggle to survive, to grow up, to make a life, to raise a family despite the scars and the nightmares. This night, for everyone present, there was no escaping what had happened in a Holocaust in a foreign land decades ago—to those who had died and to those who had survived.

The offenders had stories of their own. The young man, eighteen years old but looking only twelve, had run away from home two years earlier. He'd been abused physically and emotionally by his stepfather. He suffered from hearing loss and a speech defect. He was taunted at school. He made his way to Alabama. Members of the Aryan Nation admitted him to their school, where for months he was indoctrinated in the ways of bigotry and hate.

His education completed, he left the school and made his way back to Iowa, where he hoped to recruit and nurture his own community of neo-Nazis. His success was limited: His only recruit was the girl who fell under the spell of his vision. The two came up with a plan to spread their message and draw attention to their cause. The synagogue was a logical target.

The gulf between the experiences of the synagogue members and the teenagers was wide. But over the course of the evening, as people exchanged stories, the gulf narrowed. Self-awareness gave way to awareness of others. For the young man, pictures of Jews from photo albums he had studied at the Aryan Nation school were replaced by faces of wisdom and suffering.

The temple members, slowly at first, came to see the offenders for what they were—lost, abused, and frightened children. Early calls to "throw the book" at the two gave way to compassionate understanding that there must be a better way.

One of the Holocaust survivors asked the young man what he wanted from the temple members. He replied that he wanted forgiveness. Rabbi Fink, who had been silent for much of the evening, spoke. He said that in his tradition, the tradition of Abraham, Isaac, and Jacob, forgiveness had to be earned, and, in this instance, nothing had been done to earn it. He spoke of atonement and its importance to the Jewish community. He said that if the two were to atone for their transgressions, then—and only then—forgiveness would be possible.

And so it was in the context of atonement that the victims and the offenders came together in an effort to construct a plan to make it possible for forgiveness to be earned. The temple members wanted the two to succeed: to earn their way out of the guilt that had overtaken them that evening.

Following a dialogue befitting the tradition the synagogue honored, the victims and the offenders decided together that the two teenagers would each perform 200 hours of service—100 under the supervision of the temple's custodian and 100 hours with Rabbi Fink, meeting weekly to study Jewish and Holocaust history. Also, the temple would help the young man find a hearing specialist, he would have his Nazi tattoos removed, and both teenagers would obtain job skills, psychological assessments, and their GEDs. A second meeting would be held in six months. If the two had atoned in the manner agreed upon, forgiveness would be given, and the temple, through Rabbi Fink, would recommend that the criminal charges be dismissed.

In the best biblical tradition, it all came to pass. The young man and young woman worked hard, exceeding the expectations of the custodian and Rabbi Fink. They gained confidence in themselves as the result of their physical and intellectual labors, and from establishing new relationships. They passed their high school equivalency exams, secured employment, eventually got married and had a child. The rabbi and the custodian were invited to their wedding, which the custodian was able to attend. The temple gave the young couple a wedding gift.

Five years later, at a gathering of restorative justice practitioners, supporters, and police, Rabbi Fink held back tears while speaking of the two young offenders who had become his friends.

9.

Police-Community Relations

This chapter recounts two stories describing the use of restorative justice to improve human relations across entire communities. First is a story about how a town in Illinois used restorative circles to address the collective pain, confusion, and anguish emanating from the murder of George Floyd in 2020. Those circles and the training conducted in preparation for them led to the widespread adoption of restorative practices by residents in other contexts as well. The second story describes how a nonprofit in Washington state used restorative practices to build greater understanding and trust between its police department and several refugee communities.

The Healing Power
of Connecting Communities

Kevin Jones and Suzanne Montoya

We are restorative justice facilitators and educators; Kevin worked for the International Institute of Restorative Practices and Suzanne is the director of court services in McLean County, Illinois. Following the murder of George Floyd in 2020 by a Minneapolis police officer, the Rev. Dr. Brigitte Black, a local minister and community leader in Bloomington-Normal, Illinois, reached out to Kevin, seeking a way for community members to connect and be heard beyond protests. We recommended holding listening circles to provide a space for individuals to share their thoughts, feelings, and experiences related to systemic racism and discrimination. We ultimately partnered with the Bloomington chapter of Not in Our Town, a national organization dedicated to promoting diversity, inclusion, and understanding. Because this was unfolding during the height of COVID-19 restrictions, we held the listening sessions via Zoom.

In cooperation with Dr. Black and Not in Our Town, we sent out invitations to the community at large to register for a virtual event to discuss the Floyd murder and the anguish and anger it had touched off across the country. According to the International Institute of Restorative Practices, listening circles are a specific type of gathering—more community-oriented than the typical conference—designed to help people process an event or issue that poses a challenge or harm to their communities as a whole, whether or not they were directly involved. Unlike the usual restorative justice circles, they are not focused on problem solving, dialogue, or debating so much as empathetic listening, collective processing, and community building.

The response to our invitation was overwhelming, with 100 participants registering, such that we recruited and trained more than a dozen individuals to facilitate small breakout groups for the event. We were pleased to see that a very diverse group of residents across racial and employment sectors registered, including law enforcement, educators from elementary to higher education, nonprofit organizations, and citizens at large.

Our session began with Kevin welcoming everyone by name as they joined the call and thanking them for attending. He introduced the purpose for the gathering and then walked through the process and agenda for the evening's events. Dr. Black asked everyone to take a moment to center themselves, focus on the present, and cultivate mindfulness through deep breathing. Dr. Black and Kevin modeled asking and answering the questions that the participants would be asked to speak to in the breakout rooms:

1. What are your thoughts and feelings following the murder of George Floyd at the hands of law enforcement?
2. What is the hardest thing for you?
3. What is in your control and what can you do moving forward?

Each participant in small groups of seven was given up to two minutes to answer each question.

After small group discussions were completed, the facilitators met to quickly debrief key themes that participants felt comfortable sharing with the whole group. We were also able to have deeper conversations with some of the participants after the session to gain their insights and feedback, some of which are shared here.

One community attendee said that "connecting with others that have been experiencing the same thing I have been experiencing is

so powerful. For the first time I could feel the beginning of healing." Overwhelmed by emotions of pain, anger, and confusion by
Floyd's murder, she shared that she had hesitated to join the listening circle as she was concerned about her emotions taking over
and was unsure how to discuss and process what she was feeling.
Despite her initial reservations, she decided to step out of her comfort zone to attend.

To her surprise, the act of speaking and being listened to by
compassionate individuals from her community brought a sense
of relief and validation. As the listening circle continued, she no
longer felt isolated in her pain, but instead, she felt a deep sense of
connection and solidarity with the other participants.

A law enforcement attendee stated, "I was so anxious coming
into this space." He was concerned about being judged by other
participants because of his uniform. Despite his initial apprehen-
sion, he knew it was important to attend to have the opportunity to
express his own thoughts and feelings not only as a human being,
but as an officer of the law. As he entered the room, filled with a
diverse group of community members, he felt a wave of unease
wash over him. However, as he listened to the stories and experiences shared by those around him, he let down his guard and he
allowed himself to be vulnerable in a way he never had before.

He said, "It was so powerful to hear the experiences that individuals had with police officers, both positive and negative. It made
me happy to be able to express my own emotions and share openly
without fear of feeling attacked because of my uniform."

He continued: "As a law enforcement officer, I have a deep empathy for the members of our community who feel marginalized and
unheard. I understand the frustration and anger that many people
feel toward law enforcement, and I want to work toward building
trust and understanding between us. It's important for me to listen

to the concerns and experiences of those in our community, and to acknowledge the systemic issues that have led to feelings of injustice and inequality. I want to be a bridge between law enforcement and the community, working together to create positive change and build a safer, more inclusive society for all. I feel this experience was a great start of the commitment to working together for healing."

Another person who spoke was a longtime member of the NAACP. As a fervent advocate for racial justice from a young age, she had long fought for equality and representation for marginalized communities. She said, "For so long, I felt like my voice wasn't being heard, like my experiences and struggles were being overlooked. But now, because of my participation in this listening circle, I finally feel like my voice is being validated. It feels powerful to be able to speak my truth, to share my feelings, and know that I am not alone in this fight. I pray that this can serve as another step forward to a future where all voices are heard, and all stories are valued. I have hope that true justice and unity can be achieved."

One curious attendee said that she had come to the circle seeking diverse perspectives and opposing views that would challenge her own beliefs. As she settled into the breakout room, she felt a pang of disappointment at the lack of opportunity for a back-and-forth conversation. She had hoped to engage in meaningful debates that would broaden her understanding of the world around her. She believed that true growth and understanding could come only from hearing and engaging with viewpoints that differed from her own. She saw the listening circle as a space for dialogue, debate, and learning from one another, rather than a space solely for sharing personal truths.

In the session, Kevin gently reminded her that the listening circles were intended for participants to listen to others, to speak their truths and feel heard, rather than engaging in debates or opposition. As the circle continued, she found solace in the shared experiences and perspectives of her fellow participants, understanding that true growth and understanding could also come from the act of listening and empathizing with others.

After the event, the word spread of its value, and we continued to host listening circles as requested by the community at large. Eventually we incorporated additional topics occurring in the nation, such as preelection and postelection anxieties, COVID, and hate crimes against LGBTQ+ and Asian Americans.

A participant from a listening circle that focused on the presidential election shared a profound reflection. She recounted an "aha" moment, where she realized the intricate tapestry of stories, values, and visions that lay behind every voting choice. The diverse perspectives and personal experiences shared by her fellow participants opened her eyes to the complexity of political decision making. It was a moment of clarity and empathy, when she recognized that differences in opinions were not merely about politics but rooted in deeply held beliefs and aspirations for the nation. This realization inspired her to approach political discussions with a greater sense of understanding and respect for the multitude of voices that shape democracy.

A contributor from a listening circle focused on the impact of COVID shared her own transformative experience. Hearing the personal stories and challenges of others in her community brought her comfort and a newfound sense of empathy. She was able to see beyond the irritations of the many pandemic rules and guidelines to understand the human side of the restrictions. This realization inspired her to reach out, support others, and foster a sense of togetherness despite the physical distance that was then separating neighbors from one another.

In a listening circle focused on hate crimes targeting the LGBTQ+ community, a participant shared a moment of clarity when she recognized the deep-seated fear that many individuals in the LGBTQ+ community carry every day. Listening to the stories of discrimination, violence, and prejudice-motivated offenses faced by fellow community members opened her eyes to the magnitude of the challenges they endured. This realization ignited a passion within her to stand up, speak out, and fight against the injustices threatening her community's safety and well-being. As emotions ran high in the listening circle, an ally expressed support and empathy for the LGBTQ+ community.

Through our initial listening circle, something wonderful has happened in McLean County, Illinois. Listening circles transitioned from a reactive response to a harmful incident into a proactive use of restorative practices in multiple community settings.

Several faculty members from Illinois State University participated in that initial session as facilitators. When they returned to in-person teaching after the pandemic, they used a listening circle format for student orientations, as a means of welcome and much more. Our organization has a youth component, and several high school students joined in facilitating these as well. These young people were able to facilitate listening circles with peers and teachers at their high schools. One young person said, "In our school community, the use of listening circles with teachers has been a game changer. It's not just about sharing our thoughts and feelings, but about truly being heard and understood."

A teacher reflected that "these circles have created a space where students and teachers can come together as equals, where all voices are valued and respected. Through these conversations, we have built a foundation of trust and empathy that has transformed our relationships and fostered a sense of unity and collaboration. It's a powerful reminder that listening is not just about hearing words, but about truly connecting with one another on a deeper level."

Restorative practices have become ingrained in the local school systems, youth agencies, and juvenile justice system in McLean County. With each circle orchestrated, we continue to plant seeds of empathy, compassion, and hope, nurturing a community where every voice is not only heard but cherished, and where the power of listening becomes a catalyst for community transformation.

The Power of Circles

Dr. E. Jabali Stewart

I first encountered peacemaking circles in 2012, while I was serving as director of intercultural affairs at the Bush School, an independent K–12 school in Seattle, Washington. My experience was so powerful that thereafter my mission became embedding circles wherever possible in the school, and I've since helped to found a consulting company that brings restorative justice approaches to schools, families, churches, community organizations, police, nonprofits, and companies.

When I think about the power of the peacemaking circle process, there are so many stories of amazing and unexpected outcomes that it is hard to choose just one. I share here two stories that rise to the top.

The setting was a series of circles designed as an engagement between immigrant families, their youth, and members of the Seattle Police Department. We called the project the Immigrant Family Institute, and it was born of another pilot program that took place one year earlier called the Refugee Women's Institute, in which women who identified as refugees gathered with police department members to discuss a variety of topics. The goal was to build understanding and trust between refugee communities in our area and the Seattle Police Department. The program, the first of its kind in the nation, aimed to build a grassroots network of refugee women leaders while increasing the cultural competency of female officers in the police department.

Eventually, a collective realization set in that including the adolescent offspring of the refugee women in the conversations was necessary. The refugee women realized that they were learning things about how the legal system works in the United States that they wished their kids could hear directly. Everybody also agreed that learning more about the kids' perspective might shed light on patterns and trends among them, given that their lived experience was different from that of their parents and the police.

With this newfound knowledge, the two women who spear-headed the Refugee Women's Institute invited me to help design the Immigrant Family Institute. The program focused in particular on immigrant families that have been or could be impacted by the juvenile justice system. Specifically, it aimed to provide leadership skills to immigrant boys and girls aged ten to fourteen and to empower their parents to navigate city, legal, and education systems and to advocate for themselves. The program also aspired to help frontline Seattle Police Department officers be more culturally responsive in serving immigrant youth of color and their families. Here in Seattle, our recruitment efforts yielded primarily families from Somalia, Ethiopia, Eritrea, Cambodia, Vietnam, Colombia, and El Salvador.

My initial contribution was the introduction of peacemaking circles as a primary mode of engagement. Over an eight-week period, through the circle process we moved into deeper spaces of sharing personal experiences, convergent and divergent realities, hard truths, misconceptions, and laughter. Across the program's five-year lifespan, there have been a million "a-ha" moments, moments of deep understanding and clarification on all sides. Most of these took place during our circles.

Because restorative justice conversations are bounded by collective guidelines that call for confidentiality (and I was not able to seek permission from all the participants), I am not able to share exactly what was said. What I can tell you, though, is that immigrant and refugee adults got a chance to hear the perspective of their children like never before, which gave them deeper insight into their children's day-to-day realities, struggles, and their conceptions of home. Similarly, the youth got to hear things about their homelands from their family members they had not known or heard before, including just how much their parents had given up to relocate. At the same time, both family elders and youth got to hear the day-to-day reality of police officers, included the stress of living with uncertainty as to whether they would make it home from work. The police officers likewise got to hear from immigrant and refugee families, including stories of dealing with racism and anti-immigrant attitudes in this country. The participants recounted incidents they had experienced with police both in Seattle and in their homelands, which were often traumatic.

One year in particular, a large population of Somali women and children participated in our program. This offered a profound learning experience for many of the officers who had never heard even a smidgen of the information shared by those families. Seemingly basic norms to the families—such as the taboo against a man touching a woman of Muslim faith—was completely new information. For some officers, this shed light on how their behavior affected previous interactions, leading to incorrect conclusions such as "this woman is being noncompliant" because she refused to let a male officer touch her.

Toward the end of that year's sessions, two participating police officers approached me outside of the circle, saying, "We have something to tell you." I confess that initially I was nervous as they proceeded to tell a story of getting a call to a part of town in which there are a lot of Somali residents. They recounted how they pulled up to a scene teeming with agitated people, feeling the usual mode of engagement emerging in them. Then they both spoke of how they said to each other, "Okay, we learned all that stuff in the program; let's put it to use." They got out of their car, walked up to an elderly Somali woman who looked to be of some stature in the group, put their hands over their hearts, bowed ever so slightly, and asked, "How can we be of service to you?"

The reaction from the crowd was immediate. A stunned silence went through the crowd as everyone turned and looked at the officers in surprise. After ten minutes of conversation, the situation was resolved, and everybody went about their business. The officers got back in their car, themselves somewhat stunned by what had just happened. They attributed it all to what had come from sitting in circle with members of the Somali community.

Now, this is not to say that this will always happen or that this solves police brutality. But it is a powerful example of how when populations spend time together, getting to know each other, relationships can be much better. The additional information that is gleaned from conversation can lead to different decisions, and as we all know, our decisions shape our reality as well as the reality of others.

The second story that comes to mind occurred while I was introducing a middle school to the peacemaking circle process. During one period each week, students could either sit in circle or engage in another social engagement modality. The school was a fairly affluent one, with racial demographics that skewed heavily white. You can imagine what that does to conversations about race in the building.

But there was one mixed-race class in particular that I found absolutely amazing, and after sitting in circle for half a year with this group, I began to notice something. In restorative practices, a circle keeper is no more or less powerful than any other person in the circle. We create space for people to step into their agency as circle keepers. As that set in and the students began to pick up the act of keeping the circle, including the ceremonial aspects of the process, they increasingly raised their voices with questions. I noticed over time that the more they sat together, the more they willingly dived into topics and realms of conversation that I know they would not have otherwise.

So it was not surprising when one day students started asking very deep questions about race, including things like: How do you grapple with a racialized existence? How do you deal with music that has racial undertones given the demographic that you represent or the race that you represent? How do you understand how to be antiracist, from your point of view? It wasn't just that one circle; this occurred for the rest of the year, and it was both stunning and gratifying to see how these thirteen- and fourteen-year-olds were being so introspective and reflective about their relationship to race.

When I later went to a meeting with parents and staff members and the subject of race came up, it was shut down quickly because someone had mentioned the word "white." I sat there thinking to myself, *Wow, I just came out of a room with kids who have more skill and ability to have this conversation than their parents and teachers do.* It was clearly because the students took the time in circle to really build a safe space that they could hold such conversations in an atmosphere of trust.

This story also illustrates to me how the peacemaking circle process is not only relegated to the realms of conflict, discipline, or "justice." It is so much more than accountability. Circles can hold the human condition. The work I feel called to do—and I am committed to do—is to keep love, not accountability, at the center of my circles. Because accountability born of love is infinitely stronger than forced accountability. And if the word "love" made you flinch or feel a kind of way, I suggest you follow the middle schoolers' lead and sit in circle about it.

Acknowledgments

There are so many people who have encouraged me, assisted me, given me ideas, and prayed for this book to emerge into the world.

Special thanks go first of all to my family. I am especially grateful to my husband, Don, for his patience and understanding during the years I have spent immersed in this dream of mine. Don has been above and beyond supportive. This last few years when things finally started moving fast, the joke in our family is that he only recognizes me when he sees me from the back while sitting at my desk facing my laptop, because every evening when he comes home from work that is where he finds me.

Our children have each been supportive in their own amazing ways. Marcus has been my go-to person with all things related to computer challenges. He was my Microsoft Excel strategist. He formatted a sheet that could be duplicated for each storyteller's information so that I could keep color-coded sheets with notes tracking the status of each story and other details that made life much easier. There were so many possible stories and storytellers at so many different places in their story it would have been a nightmare otherwise. He also rigged two screens for my computer so that I could compare story versions, which was a huge help in the editing process. Our daughter, Jenifer, was my co-website designer, chief encourager, and cheerleader. I learned a lot about webpages alongside her and appreciated that she attended the most recent National Association of Community and Restorative Justice (NACRJ) conference with me in Washington, DC. Kevin, our photojournalist son, was great when I needed help with the photo design of my original website used for recruiting new storytellers and took my official author portrait.

Beyond my family, I have been blessed with so many others who have made this dream possible. Leigh Courtney was my first partner for several years. She not only edited stories but worked with me from the beginning to create a book proposal that would explain our dream of describing America's best-kept secret to potential publishers. It became most useful when we created the website with the purpose of looking for more storytellers.

When Leigh's life was changing and more stories began to come in, we discussed finding a new editor. That's when I found Max Sinsheimer. I am so appreciative of Max—not only for his encouragement throughout the times when I was looking for a publisher, but also for shaping my early stories and making them so much better when presenting to a potential publisher.

Soon after, an amazing thing happened. After chatting about the stories I was collecting with Howard Zehr, the pioneer of the American restorative justice movement, he introduced me to Diane Wachtell, executive director at The New Press. She was interested in publishing a volume of first-person stories. It wasn't just a dream anymore! I can never thank Howard enough for that introduction, for continuing to answer my occasional questions along the journey, and ultimately writing the foreword for this volume.

I really needed to find more storytellers from people I did not know. I want to thank Dr. Brenda Morrison, director of the Centre for Restorative Justice and associate professor in the School of Criminology at Simon Fraser University, for connecting me with Molly Rowan Leach at Restorative Justice on the Rise. Molly was able to recruit Howard, Kay Pranis, and Fania Davis to write endorsements for the idea of creating a book of restorative justice stories. Their assistance was immeasurable in making connections. Molly was able to broadcast a call for stories across her network of practitioners, which connected me with so many storytellers. I could never have discovered their stories without her help.

Diane Wachtell, Tanya Coke, and the whole editorial team at The New Press deserve applause for their insightful feedback, editing, and dedication to shaping this manuscript. From co-creating a new title for the book to decisions about how best to organize the stories, they were so very patient with me as a first-time author. Their intellectual camaraderie has been a constant source of inspiration.

There were so many others who were important to my being able to produce this book of stories, and so many mentors over the years. I wish I could name them all. In particular, much gratitude goes to fellow RJ authors Margaret Thorsborne and Nancy Riestenberg, who shared their expertise both of restorative justice and of having already produced books, and for saving my sanity.

Also very importantly, I am grateful to all twenty-eight storytellers. They represent dedicated restorative justice practitioners from all walks of life, people who have been harmed by crime, and those who have harmed others. All have been fundamentally changed by using restorative justice practices. They have shown how to move forward following breaches in their communities— from misunderstandings to major crimes—but also how to teach conflict resolution to our children and build stronger relationships within our schools as a result. I have been deeply moved by their stories and so honored to have been able to work together with them.

I met Kris Miner at an early NACRJ meeting in San Antonio.

She and Kay Pranis and I shared a hotel room for several days when planes were shut down due to heavy rains on the final day of the conference. We became dear friends and our friendship lasted. She was also one of those people who was a friend to so many others. Several years later, even though she was suffering from multiple myeloma, she was determined to get her story finished. The night before our final scheduled call, her daughter Kylie called to say Kris wouldn't be able to make that call. She passed away the next morning. Special thanks to Kylie Miner for her assistance and permission to use her mother's story here.

Thanks, as well, to Nancy Lewis, and Neely Upamaka for their assistance with final edits following the untimely deaths of storytellers Ted Lewis and Eric Butler. Sadly, both passed away within days of our NACRJ 2024 Conference. Our hearts are with you. It was an honor to have worked with Ted and Eric.

Every storyteller exemplifies "being the change we want to see in the world." And I do believe that together we can change the world.

NOTES

1. "The Origin and History of Brandolini's Law," https://effectiviology
.com/brandolinis-law/#The_origin_and_history_of_Brandolinis_law.

2. Jerome G. Miller, "The Debate on Rehabilitating Criminals: Is It
True That Nothing Works?" https://www.prisonpolicy.org/scans/rehab
.html.

3. "Recidivism of Prisoners Released in 24 States in 2008: A 10-Year
Follow-Up Period (2008–2018)," bjs.ojp.gov/sites/g/files/xyckuh236/files
/media/document/rpr24s0810yfup0818_sum.

4. Robert Balfanz, Vaughan Byrnes, and Joanna Fox, "Sent Home
and Put Off-Track: The Antecedents, Disproportionalities, and Consequences of Being Suspended in the Ninth Grade" (April 6, 2013),
civilrightsproject.ucla.edu/resources/projects/center-for-civil-rights
-remedies/school-to-prison-folder/state-reports.

5. Rather than use essentializing language like "offender" and "victim,"
some restorative justice practitioners often use the terms "harmdoer,"
"harmed person," or "harmed parties."

6. Lindsay Fulham, Julie Blais, and Elizabeth Schultheis, "The Effectiveness of Restorative Justice Programs: A Meta-Analysis of Recidivism
and Other Relevant Outcomes," *Sage Journals* (November 2023), journals
.sagepub.com/doi/10.1177/17488958231215228.

7. Sean Darling-Hammond, "Fostering Belonging, Transforming
Schools: The Impact of Restorative Practices," Learning Policy Institute
(May 2023) ("Schools that increased use of restorative practices saw a
decrease in schoolwide misbehavior, substance abuse, and student mental
health challenges, as well as improved school climate and student achieve-

ment."),learningpolicyinstitute.org/product/impact-restorative-practices
-report.

8. Precious Skinner-Osel and Peter Claudius Osei, "Integrating Restorative Justice Principles into Reentry Programs and Recidivism Measures Using the C.A.R.E. Model," *Journal of Human Behavior in the Social Environment* (November 2024), doi.org/10.1080/10911359.202
4.2434699.

9. Ana Nascimento, Joana Andrade, and Andrea de Castro Rodrigues, "The Psychological Impact of Restorative Justice Practices on Victims of Crimes—a Systematic Review," pmc.ncbi.nlm.nih.gov/articles/PMC10240635.

10. Will Bledsoe, *The Restorative Way: Harnessing the Power of Restorative Communication to Mend Relationships, Heal Trauma, and Reclaim Civility One Conversation at a Time* (Fort Collins, CO: Restorative Way Inc., 2024).

11. After this teacher was removed, he called me late at night, insinuating he would cause me physical harm. After that I always carried a pocketknife, a small solace but also a reminder to watch my surroundings, especially because I often entered and exited the school building with no other people around, late at night and on the weekends. He wasn't the only person that made physical threats, with one teacher threatening, "I'll send thugs to beat up your pregnant wife." A couple students and parents similarly made threats, with at least one father having to be held back by my assistant principal.

12. Judith Lewis Herman, *Truth and Repair: How Trauma Survivors Envision Justice* (New York: Basic Books, 2023).

13. Alissa Ackerman and Jill S. Levenson, *Healing from Sexual Violence: The Case for Vicarious Restorative Justice* (Brandon, VT: Safer Society Press, 2019).

About the Editor

Sally Swarthout Wolf has more than twenty years of experience as a restorative justice practitioner, trainer, speaker, and leader. She is the former director of Ford County Probation and Court Services and the co-founder of the Illinois Balanced and Restorative Justice Project. She lives in Paxton, Illinois.

Publishing in the Public Interest

Thank you for reading this book published by The New Press; we hope you enjoyed it. New Press books and authors play a crucial role in sparking conversations about the key political and social issues of our day.

We hope that you will stay in touch with us. To keep up to date with our books, events, and the issues we cover, follow us on social media and sign up for our newsletter at thenewpress.org.

Please consider buying New Press books not only for yourself, but also for friends and family and to donate to schools, libraries, community centers, prison libraries, and other organizations involved with the issues our authors write about.

The New Press is a 501(c)(3) nonprofit organization; if you wish to support our work with a tax-deductible gift please visit https://thenewpress.org/donate/ or use the QR code below.